REAL ESTATE A WOMAN'S WORLD

MARY SHERN

The Saga of Suzy Soldsine, Super Salesperson

REAL ESTATE EDUCATION COMPANY

International Standard Book Number: 0-88462-373-4
Copyright 1979 by Development Systems Corporation
Published by Real Estate Education Company/Chicago

10 9 8 7 6 5 4 3 2 1

Cover design by Joan Johns and Alfred T. Furtado
Illustrations by Alfred T. Furtado

Dedication

I wish to acknowledge a debt of gratitude to the Real Estate Education Company for having encouraged me to do this book and for having put up with my personal time management problems (see chapter 7!). One person in particular has worked so closely as to have become like a daughter to me—critical, sassy, and obtrusive—and also, on many occasions, absolutely right. For all her hard work and many constructive suggestions, and also for having led me to a deli that serves the nation's best chopped liver, I dedicate this book to its editor, Ruth Silverman.

Contents

Preface

Space prevents acknowledging contributions from the literally hundreds of women in various realms of real estate who have enriched this book with experiences, ideas, thoughts, and anecdotes. However, since the sum total remains at least partially autobiographical, it seems only fair to note my own qualifications and prejudices.

"Woman" is a status I've enjoyed for 58 years. No use fibbing about it since assorted relatives and progency proclaim the number from the housetops on every natal day and create fire-hazard alerts with the candles on the cake. Whether it's the sex I would have chosen will have to remain beside the point until science affords us the luxury of selection. On the rare occasions (picnics, for example) when I catch myself wishing I had been born a male I suppress the thought and embrace the status quo with enthusiasm.

"Married" is a title I acquired entirely by choice after a whirlwind wartime romance in 1943. The old biddies who sat in the front of the church and muttered that it could never last will at least have to admit that we made it through the first 35 years. Long ago in college, I heard a speaker suggest that girls should marry right after high school and then later, when their children are grown, pursue education and careers. It's hard to say which image was more unattractive to me—the 17-year-old mother or the 40-year-old sophomore. However, in the dormitory gab sessions when girls of that era pondered the seemingly inevitable choice between marriage and a career, I determined with all the greed of youth to have both, either concurrently or consecutively. Have them I did, and no one has ever convinced me that one detracts from the other in any major respect, some plus and minus factors notwithstanding.

"Mother" is a name I've earned so often that there was once a time when we suspected the obstetrician had me filed under Y for "You again." Our four daughters and three sons represent an affront to zealous advocates of zero population growth, but since they're all "keepers," we humbly accept our share of blame for traffic jams, crowded beaches, and declining natural resources. Although certifiably lacking in any other domestic virtue, I've loved the challenge of raising my children and find it infinitely rewarding despite all the headaches and heartaches. The big event of my year is the annual family reunion, which now includes sons- and daughters-in-law and grandchildren and begins to take on the appearance (and decibels) of a political convention.

"Real estate broker" represents for me a somewhat surprising career choice, since I started out as a writer and performer in the radio-television industry. To be in real estate is to experience total immersion. If one stays, it must be something more than a career and closer to a flaming love affair. In my case, the affair has endured for more than a quarter-century. It has dealt me a fair share of bruises but also myriad satisfactions. I cherish lasting friendships with clients and fellow Realtors, and the achievement of goals ranging from the frivolous to the sublime. Although I resist equating success with dollars, I might add that real estate has supported my latent passion for sinful luxuries and sustained me through such whims as collecting crystal, cars, and condominiums.

Real estate can indeed be called a woman's world, not only because women are the backbone of the sales force, but also because their traditional role in society is an asset. Our profession might truly be the last bastion of free enterprise. Typically, salespeople manage their own careers, and profit to the extent of their own achievements. Even before the advent of the feminine mystique, women participated on the same payscale as men. Nothing impeded their rise to success, not even the most died-in-the-wool male chauvinist you-know-what. (Perhaps that statement should be limited to real estate brokerage. There are still tales of sexual discrimination in related professions, such as mortgage lending, title search, escrow, and so on.) As the old saying goes—in most businesses a woman must perform twice as well as a man to a achieve success—and fortunately, it's easy. In real estate she need only be an equal performer, a task about as difficult as getting a Democratic politician to vote the straight ticket.

"Militant feminist" I am not, nor, in fact, militant anything. Although capable of some fairly aggressive behavior in a sales situation (motivation, y'know), I still cringe when returning unsatisfactory merchandise to the local department store or a wrinkled shirt to the laundry. I view all "causes" with about the same attitude I feel toward kidney stones—abject terror.

The concept of equal pay for equal work sounds only fair, but I've never aspired to be a fireman or front-line soldier, to join a men's club, to use the men's washroom, to wear men's clothes, or even to don Bella Abzug's hats. My bras were never for burning. My psyche doesn't cringe when I'm called a "salesman"; I find the term "chairperson" pretty ridiculous; and I hooted with laughter when recently I received a letter with the salutation "Dear Gentleperson."

I fail to become upset over the shifting sands of sexual roles in society. I choose my role and let others do the same. In real estate, we can pursue our course *because* we're women, not in spite of it, and do our task without losing an ounce of femininity. Therefore, I more or less oppose equal rights. Why should women give up the edge we've so richly deserved and so long enjoyed?

Please read into these chapters no rancor for men. I discovered a liking for men at an early stage of puberty, and the feeling has only deepened throughout the years. I gratefully acknowledge that a major share of credit for my success belongs to two magnificent men. My father firmly believed that all girls should have a vocation to "fall back on" and fought for my right to higher education against a Southern mother who sincerely felt that her responsibilities to her daughters must culminate in a proper debut. My husband not only tolerated my career aspirations but also taught me most of what I know about real estate. He has aided, abetted, pushed, prodded, and even bankrolled me with confidence that on occasion has far exceeded his common sense.

Like so many thousands of other Americans, I am woman, wife, mother, and Realtor. God forbid that the lighthearted story of Suzy Soldsine would cause readers to doubt my humble gratitude and deep respect for each and every one of these roles. My life is demanding, exciting, rewarding, and satisfying. It's also fun, and the laughs seemed worth sharing.

1
Choosing a Career – or Vice Versa

It would be inaccurate to say that Suzy Soldsine chose a career in real estate. People don't choose real estate careers. It tends to be the other way around. True, there may be a few children here and there who confidently plan to grow up and become real estate brokers. These are obviously oddballs and, therefore, more likely to study psychiatry. Ask any group of Realtors® and you'll find that, typically, they came into the field quite by accident. They needed a job either for the money, for the challenge, just to pass the time, or for any combination of these three. At that critical moment, someone just happened to suggest real estate. Since no other alternative cropped up that looked interesting or for which they felt remotely qualified, the suggestion became an inspiration.

Suzy's history was not so different from that of many other women she knew. Years before, she'd made the smooth and proper transition from pom-poms to pablum with only a brief stopover in swinging singlehood. Since John had a good job with a local road construction firm, there was never a question of Suzy having to work. Never the time, either.

By the time Suzy had mastered curtain hanging and soft-boiling eggs, Mike had arrived. The Soldsines adored their firstborn. They adjusted their lives to naptime and feeding schedules and breathed a sigh of relief when Mike could finally feed and pot himself. Then came Erin, who was quick to walk. She was also quick to develop a passion for climbing to precarious heights and an appetite for dead flies and wallpaper. The need for eternal vigilance persisted even after Joey joined the family.

So far, life had brought Suzy everything mother had promised it would—a loving husband, wonderful children, a brick home in the suburbs with a two-car garage. Suzy learned to cope, little knowing how invaluable that talent was to become.

Suzy's crisis came when Joey, her youngest, started to school. After years of complaining that she never had a moment to herself, not even in the bathtub, she was alone in the house—and lonely.

Marjorie, a neighbor in similar circumstances, came over to share coffee, misery, and the problem of how to fill their newfound free time. They spoke in whispers, of course, so that the other neighborhood mothers who where still hip deep in toddlers wouldn't hear and summon the nearest shrink.

"It'll be heaven to go shopping without the kids underfoot," Marjorie suggested. "We can go to luncheons and movies . . ."

"Maybe even join a card club," Suzy added with a touch of sarcasm.

"Great idea! I've been meaning to brush up on my bridge."

"Marjorie, that's just what I don't want—spending my afternoons with a bunch of women, chitchatting about husbands and children and broadleaf philodendrons . . ."

"What's so bad about that?" Marjorie interrupted, bristling. "God knows the men love talking about their jobs. I'm not ashamed of being a homemaker."

"Of course not," Suzy replied, soothingly. "But there's got to be more to life. Last night at dinner I had the scary feeling I was beginning to sound like a Crest commercial."

"You could have switched to detergents," Marjorie laughed.

"Besides, those card-club sharks play for blood, you know."

"I'll say! Three strawberry daiquiris and I can never remember what's trump."

Then, Suzy and Marjorie briefly kicked around and dismissed the idea of taking up a hobby. Although in awe of women who can turn old flour sacks into attractive tea cozies, Suzy suffered from an abysmal lack of artistic talent. Any desire that she might have had to ply a needle was more than fulfilled by the weekly knee-patching, seasonal hem-letting-down, and constant button-stitching her family demanded. Her attempts at gardening were of necessity confined to a few species that supposedly can't be killed. She'd often proved that contention to be in error. Sports, in her humble opinion, were designed for people who enjoy panting, perspiration, and pain. She was hardpressed to perform even such mundane activities as getting into the backseat of a two-door car gracefully or snapping the crotch on her body suit. Furthermore, she had already tried and discarded astrology, yoga, transcendental meditation, and health foods (alfalfa gave her gas).

Marjorie left, but Suzy's mind was still spinning. Quietly and tenaciously the idea of getting a job crept into her thinking. With it came several pressing problems. How would John react to the suggestion that his wife seek employment? His comments could vary all the way from "It's about time" to "How dare you imply that I can't provide for my family." Worse still, the latter sentiment would probably remain unvocalized, surfacing obliquely as moodiness, pouting, and tantrums, and causing a marital climate akin to the coming of the New Ice Age.

And, what about the children? Would their lives be blighted if they ate cornflakes for breakfast instead of hot oatmeal? Would they become dropouts if she weren't always on hand to dole out peanut butter sandwiches at the end of the school day? Suzy had already experienced guilt attacks, the occupational disease of parenthood, on the few occasions when she'd been unable to be there when her children needed her. She was well aware that the small print in the marriage contract makes guilt-bearing woman's work. That's something a woman knows instinctively, without ever being told or shown.

Furthermore, what about the household—still her primary responsibility? Would her so-called free time be adequate to take on a job? Could she preserve her health and sanity wearing two hats, or would life become a schizophrenic nightmare?

Finally, what would people think? (If Suzy hadn't brought that to mind herself, mother would surely have mentioned it.) Herein lies one of life's mysteries: when junior falls off the monkey bars and breaks a bone, and mother can't be reached because she's at a matinee, that's OK; but if mother can't be reached because she's making an honest dollar, it's definitely not OK. Out of economic necessity, the working wife has become a fact of life in America. But in Suzy's comfortable circle, a job would make her a maverick. Some people would say she was neglecting her husband, children, stove, and mending basket and, therefore, could be held responsible for a philandering husband, a juvenile delinquent, and an assortment of other social evils, not to mention unemployment.

It then occurred to Suzy that a part-time job was the ideal compromise. Then she could say, "Of course I'm always home when the children get out of school." Unfortunately, a surreptitious perusal of the want ads revealed that part-time employers were few in number and offered such goodies as telephone soliciting in your home, envelope addressing in your home, and cleaning up after the animals when the circus is in town. All were equally unattractive.

The want ads also contained a tiresome repetition of certain phrases such as "Must be experienced" and "No beginners." It was a devastating revelation that employers value skills and experience above personality and good intentions. Realistically, Suzy knew she couldn't type, take shorthand, keep books, or file, and she had no desire to attain such abilities. Her previous work experience consisted of having been a soda jerk during high school, wherein she set an enviable record for consumption of maraschino cherries. Later, there was a brief tenure in an expensive ladies dress shop. That came to a screeching halt the day Suzy asked an obnoxious lady with a size 14 body and a size 10 dress in her hand if she were out of her ever-lovin' mind. So much for skill and experience.

"I've been thinking about getting a job," Suzy told Marjorie when they met again.

The grass is always . . .

. . . greener!

"Yea, me too," Marjorie responded. "But nine-to-five is just impossible. And besides, where would we look?"

"Mmmmmm. *Where* is the question, all right. How far do you think I can go on blue eyes and naturally curly hair?"

"You're too modest, Suzy. Remember the PTA bake sale. You unloaded everything in an hour-and-a-half."

"Doesn't take much imagination to sell cupcakes to hungry 10-year-olds."

"Still, I'll bet you could sell. You could sell anything—a curling iron to Kojak."

"Sell? Sure, why not?" Suzy replied, mulling it over.

"Hey! I've got it!" Marjorie exclaimed. "Why don't the two of us open a boutique?"

"A gift shop?"

"An anything shop. Whatever strikes our fancy." Marjorie was pleased with her brainstorm, and Suzy caught her enthusiasm.

"I like it, Marjorie. I really do. But it'll take some planning."

In an air of suppressed excitement and delicious conspiracy, the partners devoted 2 full months to scientific research. They combed the shopping centers for the best location and agonized over whether the decor should be green and white or beige and burgundy. Stoically, they agreed to take turns making buying trips to New York, London, and Paris. In due time, the plan was ready for submission to their husbands. They arranged to have cocktails together and took care to choose the most propitious moment, right after the second well-chilled martini. The men were merciless.

"Have you any idea how much money it takes to start a business?"

"Where's the money coming from?"

"What about the legal requirements? The tax consequences? The insurance?"

"What do you know about percentage leases?"

"Who's supposed to do the housework while you're running the store?"

Suzy began to have the uncomfortable feeling that this was a quiz and she was flunking. She managed to keep her cool until her husband provided the last straw.

"If you have so much free time on your hands," he suggested, "why don't you try volunteer work?"

That did it! Suzy pointed out that she had been an alter lady, a United Fund solicitor, and a director of the woman's club. She also reminded him that she was allergic to incense, had been bitten by the Smithfields' dog, and was forced to spend hours debating whether or not to rosebud the radishes at the annual luncheon. Warming up to the subject, she added that she had been a class mother, a den mother, and a playground mother. Also Mike's mother, Erin's mother, Joey's mother, and, come to think of it, John's wife. What she hadn't been for too many years was Suzy.

"It isn't a question of wiling away idle hours," she cried. "I want an identity, my own pocket money, and my own victories."

"I don't know, Suzy. If the men don't approve of this . . ." Marjorie began.

Suzy was not to be stopped. "I'm not prepared to get all my kicks for the rest of my life beaming over John's promotions or Mike's merit badges!"

Surprised at the depth of her own feelings, Suzy burst into tears. John supplied the Kleenex, made reassuring sounds, and helped himself to another martini. After Marjorie and her husband left, Suzy apologized for her outburst.

"I understand where you're coming from honey," John said soothingly. "You don't want to be shackled to the crock pot. The boutique idea's too ambitious, but . . ."

"But you don't object to a working wife?" Suzy asked eagerly.

"It'll take some getting used to. Find something that's not going to cost me more than your tennis lessons and I'll try to adapt."

The stage was now set for some well-meaning friend to suggest that Suzy try real estate. Where such suggestions originate is one of the greatest unsolved mysteries of the real estate profession—obviously, they come not from people who have tried it. Suzy was told it would be an ideal career for a homemaker. She'd be her own boss, work only when it was convenient, meet lots of interesting people, and make a scandalous amount of money. She was assured that she had outstanding qualifications: namely, good looks, a liking for houses, and a modest talent for interior decorating. It sounded plausible, especially when Suzy recalled the agent from whom she had bought her own house and who had earned $3,000 in the process, despite being fat, frumpy, and guilty of misspelling four words on a simple offer.

After the boutique debacle, Suzy was reluctant to spring the new plan on John until she had pretested it. Somewhat to her surprise, she found that nearly everyone has some intimate knowledge of real estate.

"It's like catching a disease," Suzy told Marjorie. "You know . . . the doctor tells you that you have 'Fogerty's Syndrome,' and you've never heard of it. But soon as you tell someone, you find out that everyone has either had it or knows someone who has. Seems nearly everyone I know has had a case of 'real estate.'"

To be truthful, the input wasn't altogether optimistic and encouraging. The notion that it really isn't hard work and takes up very little time elicited some hysterical laughter. Employing brokers were characterized as a mean breed, tending to play favorites, keeping the best clients for themselves, and on occasion even expecting salespeople to go out and ring doorbells. The market was described as capricious, with abundant listings to be had when there were no buyers and multitudes of buyers when there were no listings. Commissions were defined as income that never materializes when you really need it, and some unkind soul noted that out-of-pocket expenses can be considerable. Clients were often known to be difficult, unreasonable, and prone to take up great blocks of time although they intended all along to buy through their brothers-in-law. Worst of all was the considered opinion that society rates salespeople only slightly above cattle thieves and child molesters.

Despite the discouragement, Suzy held to the plan. There are, after all, two routes to satisfying careers—the grand and glorious opportunity route and the what-have-I-got-to-lose-nothing-else-has-turned-up-anyway route. Suzy was already accustomed to oven·cleaning, sibling rivalries, and overflowing septic tanks—so how tough could it be to show a house?

This time, Suzy sprung the idea on John in a fairly offhand way. Over the morning coffee and when he was deeply engrossed in the morning paper, she remarked, "I've been talking to Eloise about going into real estate. She loves it and thinks I'd do fine."

Without so much as a ripple, John replied, "Fine, why not?"

"Of course, I'd only be part-time," Suzy continued.

John was absorbed in the Dow-Jones averages, and Suzy knew she could have announced that she had decided to become a missionary in Botswana or a hit man for the Mafia and gotten the same response. Later, when the message finally sank in, he muttered dire predictions that taxes and babysitters would cost more than she could earn. However, since no significant opposion was mounted, the die was cast. Suzy had chosen real estate—or vice versa.

READER'S QUIZ

This is a guaranteed foolproof quiz. All answers are correct. Give yourself a mark of 100, and brag a lot.

1.   The thought of pursuing a career first occurred to me when

    _____ a.   my mother-in-law moved in.
    _____ b.   my unemployment compensation ran out.
    _____ c.   my husband retired and began to hang around the house.
    _____ d.   I met a good-looking broker.
    _____ e.   other

2. Real estate was suggested to me by

_____ a.   a friend who had tried it with outstanding success.
_____ b.   an enemy who had tried it and failed.
_____ c.   a broker who admired my figure.
_____ d.   restless creditors.
_____ e.   other

3. Real estate appealed to me because

_____ a.   it seemed like a way to work and still have lots of time at home.
_____ b.   it seemed like a good excuse for getting out of my home.
_____ c.   it afforded me a chance to talk to people over 10 years of age.
_____ d.   it gave me a reason to buy a car.
_____ e.   other

4. I felt confident that brokers would be impressed by the fact that I had formerly been

_____ a.   a Tupperware hostess.
_____ b.   a cheerleader.
_____ c.   a go-go dancer.
_____ d.   a lady wrestler.
_____ e.   other

5. The reaction of my husband (father, boyfriend, and so on) was

_____ a.   "Are you out of your mind? You tried Avon and couldn't even give away free samples."
_____ b.   "If you think that means I'm doing dishes, you'd better think again."
_____ c.   "Let me know when I can retire in the manner to which I'd like to become accustomed."
_____ d.   "If it leaves you less time for shopping, I'm all for it."
_____ e.   other

2
New License + New Job =New Wardrobe

A license is defined as an official authorization to engage in a business, occupation, or activity. Generally, one needs a license in order to practice medicine, dentistry, law, accountancy, or stock brokerage. Some states also require licenses for barbers, bartenders, artificial inseminators, fish-bait dealers, masseurs, pedicurists, and rainmakers, to name just a few.

In theory, licensing protects the consumer. After all, license applicants must prove their competency by mastering the state's required course of study and conquering the licensing examination. This system does sometimes fall short of perfection, which can be seen by correlating the licensing of automobile drivers with the mayhem on the highways.

The prerequisites for licensing are hammered out in the hallowed halls of the state bureaucracy. Each occupation is regulated by its own state agency, a system that often results in strange inconsistencies. For example, in one state, a barber who gives $6-haircuts has to study three times as many hours to get his license as a real estate agent who sells $90,000-homes. Why? Because that's what the law says.

Even within a single profession, the licensing requirements differ widely from state to state. In some, the aspiring real estate salesperson must study as many as 60 hours before taking the licensing examination. In her state, Suzy was required only to pass the test.

Having made the decision to embark on a real estate career, Suzy felt her first step should be to acquire some suitable clothes. Her daily wardrobe was the typical homemaker's uniform—housecoats, jeans, t-shirts, and busted-out tennis shoes. Anything that was too small for John, too big for the children, too good for Goodwill, or not quite ragged enough for the ragbag automatically gravitated toward her closet. It was fine for fingerpainting or hosing down the driveway but far removed from *Vogue*'s concept of the professional woman.

"Hold it," John protested, "you won't need the clothes till you have a job, and you can't get a job till you have a license."

"And I can't get the license till I pass the exam," Suzy added.

"I wouldn't worry about that," John assured her. "There are

about 12,000 real estate agents in this state. You can't tell me they're all eggheads. Offhand, I can think of a few who fall right between dull-normal and borderline retarded.

This reminded Suzy of their last ski trip. John had taken her to the top of the lift and said, "Push off, Suzy. How can it be dangerous? All those little kids are doing it."

Suzy, in her innocence, had pushed off. And where had that gotten her? Straight into traction. On the subject of real estate examinations, she decided to seek another opinion.

A neighbor, Barbie, proved to be a fountain of reliable information, since she had taken the real estate exam the previous month . . . also the month before that and the month before that. Predictably, her remarks did little to inspire Suzy's confidence. Barbie had found the questions to be tricky, difficult, confusing, ambiguous, and flat-out unfair. What was infinitely worse, some of the questions were mathematical.

"Eloise has a license," Suzy protested. "She thought the exam was easy."

"Eloise got her license years ago, "Barbie explained, "probably right after the San Francisco quake."

"So," Suzy said, "she still had to pass the test."

"It was easy then. You were a winner if you could write your own name—with no points off for misspelling." It was Barbie's considered opinion that at one time licenses might have been given away as prizes in boxes of Cracker Jacks. "Now," she continued, "they expect you to understand Einstein's theory, new math, and even how to fill out income tax forms."

Thus intimidated, Suzy decided to take a real estate course. The phone book listed dozens of schools, so Suzy covered her eyes and pointed. The first one she called offered free enrollment. Free, that is, if she would agree to sign a 3-year, 90-page contract with Repulsive Realty. After a few more calls, Suzy was thoroughly confused. All the schools assured her that 92.4 percent of their students passed the state license examination. None offered any guarantee, however, and no one could explain the 7.6 percent failure rate or even describe what six-tenths of a person looks like. Suzy finally opted for a medium-priced school with a convenient location and an instructor who sounded compassionate. That it was *not* the school Barbie had attended was a definite plus.

The textbook closely resembled the Manhattan telephone directory. Suzy inspected it with certain trepidation. Was she supposed to digest it by the page or the pound? Clearly, it would be tough going for someone whose current reading was more along the lines of "Jane sees Dick," and "Look, Dick, see Jane." The book was totally and depressingly devoid of sex, humor, or violence. It could be depended upon in any 20 minutes of concentrated application to render sleeping pills obsolete.

The real estate students were a mixed bag at best. They came in all ages and sizes and from every profession and vocation imaginable. But the class soon developed a close-knit camaraderie, dusting off long-unused study skills to learn a bewildering number of words in a mysterious language called "legalese." They all agreed that a *fee simple* is not simple at all, nor is an *easement* ever easy. Together, the students agonized through weekly quizzes and the sadistic practice of posting the results.

Suzy had graduated from high school with a major in sock hops, cheerleading, and recess. When she donned her cap and gown, both parents breathed audible sighs of relief. College was never even mentioned. Now, to her surprise, Suzy found the schoolwork interesting and stimulating despite painful struggles and mediocre grades. She was particularly drawn to those students who shared her distaste for math. Honesty compels noting that the majority of these were women.

"It's exactly what Mike's studying in eighth grade," John said when he looked at her workbook.

"I know, and don't you dare show him my grades," Suzy replied. "The kids are having enough laughs over mommy doing her homework. Erin wants to know if my teacher is pretty, and Joey asked if I'd gotten any gold stars yet."

"Women can calculate as well as men," John went on. "They just don't get the day-to-day practice."

"Maybe we'd rather not," Suzy laughed. "It's like changing a tire—if you don't learn, you won't have to."

"How could you possibly sell real estate if you can't calculate mortgage payments, taxes, or closing costs—and, of course, commissions."

"Oh, I'll manage," Suzy sighed. "But it's painful. God bless calculators and payment tables!"

"You're pretty anxious about this exam, aren't you?" John asked.

"*Terrified* is a better word." Suzy replied.

"Try to stay cool, Suzy," John suggested. "Remember your driver's license test? You knew how to drive perfectly well, but you blew it by being so uptight."

"Thanks a lot for bringing that up again!" Suzy shouted. "I did just fine on that stupid road test except for cutting one corner a little close. A charitable inspector would've overlooked it."

"I'd say running through a lawn, a rose garden, and a picket fence was cutting it more than a little close," John chortled. It was one of his most cherished recollections.

The exam day finally dawned, if "dawn" is the proper word to use about a day that comes in gray and drizzly on the heels of a sleepless night. The group assembled in a high school classroom that should have been condemned, if, in fact, it hadn't been. It was equipped with an inadequate air conditioner, undersized seats, and a proctor who bore a startling resemblance to the Wicked Witch of the West. Suzy was buzz-bombed by a hostile insect and seated across from a mutterer.

"*A, only I is true—B, only II is false . . .*"

In spite of that, she muddled through and even felt pretty confident. Confident, that is, until the examinees gathered outside afterward.

"What did you get for number 57?"

"All of the above. Didn't you?"

"I put *a.*"

"How about that insurance proration?"

With maddening regularity, the consensus deemed the correct answer to be the one Suzy hadn't chosen. By the time she got home, Suzy was ready to accept defeat and take in either laundry or a good, stiff drink. She settled for the drink.

Now began the ordeal of waiting for results. On the day the envelope arrived, Suzy had already suffered a headache, a child who woke up with a rash that would almost certainly prove to be chicken pox, runs in three pairs of pantyhose, and a broken fingernail. The envelope lay on the table for 2 hours before she dared open it. Then, wonder of wonders, that single, magnificent word—Suzy had *passed.*

Next came the task (well, after the chicken pox epidemic) of choosing a company. From the ads she read and the letters she received, Suzy was led to believe that dozens of real estate companies were waiting to welcome new licensees with warmth, tenderness, and unlimited opportunity. Instead, she discovered that job hunting in real estate is just like job hunting in anything else—a masochistic experience designed to reduce one's ego to the size of a rust spot on a pin.

Suzy couldn't even line up an interview. Being an honest woman, she said she was looking for a part-time position. Her first three calls were abruptly terminated. Only full-time people were being accepted. This called for advice from Eloise, who had for some time been combining a career in real estate with marriage, singing in the choir, politics, volunteer work, and assorted Amway franchises.

"Eloise!" Suzy cried into the phone, "you said I could spend as much or as little time as I wanted in real estate. But no one's hiring part-timers! What gives?"

"You just don't understand the language," Eloise said soothingly. *"Full-time* and *part-time* are just words. They don't have anything to do with time, but whether or not you have another job. If you work 40 hours a week for the telephone company and put in 50 hours on real estate, you're part-time. If you work only 10 hours a week on real estate but haven't any other job, you're full-time. Got it?"

"No, I'm still confused," Suzy moaned. "Isn't homemaking a job?"

"You might think so, and I might think so, but brokers don't look at it that way," Eloise assured her. "You're definitely full-time, and that's that."

That hurdle out of the way, Suzy turned back to the want ads. Her next phone call did elicit an interview. Like most job interviews, Suzy's began with an application. After 15 minutes of trying to fill it out, Suzy was convinced the form had been designed by a sadist who got his (or her) kicks thinking up questions that can't be interpreted and asking for information no one could possibly recall.

The first questions were easy and lulled Suzy into a false sense of security. She had no problem with *name, address, telephone number, marital status,* and so on. Then, up popped *other names used.*

"Do they want my maiden name? Nickname? Alias?" she puzzled.

Residence for the last 10 years with addresses and dates called for improvision, and as for *previous employment,* she hadn't the faintest idea when or for how long she'd worked at the soda fountain, nor, for that matter, whether she'd ever had measles or mumps.

"Who cares?" she thought. "And why is my mother's maiden name so important?"

By the time she reached the lines for listing personal references, Suzy's mind was a blank. She was horrified to find herself writing down the name of a shirttail relative of the black sheep variety, currently serving 5-to-10 for embezzlement. The address was, of course, inappropriate.

But the worst was yet to come. The form provided ample space for writing small essays on a number of challenging themes.

Why do you want to sell real estate?

(How do I know if I'll want to or not 'till I've tried?)

What can you contribute to our business?

(Frankly, I'm a little more concerned about what you can contribute to me.)

What do you think your earnings will be 2 years from now?

(How about leaving that 'till we see how the first year goes.)

"High schools should give courses in filling out forms," Suzy stewed. "Who cares if I know when the Battle of the Little Bighorn was fought? Or how much President Whatsis paid for Louisiana?"

The application became the basis for the questions in the ensuing interview. At least that's what Suzy assumed from the way the broker was scowling over it when she was ushered into his office. She was offered a comfortable chair, a fleeting smile, and a dreadful cup of coffee. Then, the questions began, and it was more of the same only worse, because she didn't have time to think. The interview went something like this:

BROKER: Tell me about yourself, Suzy. What are you good at?

SUZY: Well, I'm a wife and a mother and that's about it. Everyone says I make terrific lasagna.

BROKER: What awards or blue ribbons have you won?

SUZY: I don't exactly need a trophy room, ha ha, if that's what you mean.

BROKER: What are your needs? What do you want to get out of your career?

SUZY: It isn't a question of needs, actually. My husband is doing just fine in his career. He gives us everything we want. I just want to be busy, and, of course, I wouldn't have trouble thinking of ways to spend extra money.

BROKER: What ways?

SUZY: Offhand, I can't think.

BROKER: What do you expect to be, say, 5 years from now?

SUZY: Five years older—that's for sure.

BROKER: What can you do for us, Suzy? I mean, what can you give us besides dollars?

SUZY: (coldly) I'm not sure how to interpret that question.

Suzy was conscious of sounding like the village idiot. She wasn't surprised when the broker said that there were no openings at the present time. He gently explained that a selling career requires a great deal of motivation and that wives who don't have to worry about the rent usually aren't inclined to work very hard. Suzy departed, not without doubts about the view that women will work for bread, butter, and beans, but not for pearls, Porsches, and prime beef.

After that disastrous interview, Suzy humbly decided to ask John for help, as his job included interviewing applicants for clerical and secretarial positions.

"I need a few pointers about this silly interview business," she told him that evening.

"Well," John began, "I think the worst thing you can do is chew gum; it makes a terrible impression."

"Be serious, John," she interrupted. "You know perfectly well that I never chew gum."

"How about posture, then? You do have a habit of slumping, Suzy. It detracts from an image of alertness and interest."

With growing impatience, Suzy politely informed him that there's no way you can sit up straight in a low-slung, overstuffed chair.

"I don't know then," John mused, "unless you asked for too much money. Employers can't pay more than the job is worth."

"The subject of money never even came up," she said, "except that the broker did ask what I expected to be earning 2 years from now."

"And what did you say?"

"That I hadn't the faintest idea," she replied.

"I must say that doesn't sound overly bright."

"Tell me, oh Guru, what magic number should I have mentioned?"

"Guess I'd have to give that some thought. Did he give a reason for not taking you on?"

"Yes," Suzy replied, "he said that wives of successful husbands usually aren't motivated to work very hard."

John swelled visibly. "Undoubtedly speaks from experience. Maybe these are facts you're going to have to face."

Luckily for John, the telephone interrupted them at that precise moment. Eloise was calling to say she'd heard that FFC (Foley, Feinberg, and Chong) Realty Corp. were desperate for new salespeople and were hiring anyone who could demonstrate the ability to breathe in and out. The company name was only vaguely familiar to Suzy, but if FFC was truly what Eloise referred to as a "body shop," then they were worth a call. They certainly had an admirable personnel policy.

FFC not only presented her with an application to fill out but they also administered a psychological test. There were 175 multiple-choice questions, and at least 150 of these had no appropriate answer. She found herself nostalgically yearning for a good old "none of the above." No such luck. For example:

- It would be interesting to be

    a.   a performer.
    b.   a bridge builder.
    c.   uncertain

(If I have never had the slightest desire to be a performer or a bridge builder, must I then find it interesting to be an uncertain?)

- When someone becomes very angry with me, I

    a.   try to calm him or her down.
    b.   get irritated.
    c.   become confused.

(It all depends on whether it's a husband, child, friend, or cleaning lady.)

- When people are pushy, I do just the opposite of what they want

    a.   yes
    b.   in between
    c.   no

(How many people? How big?)

Suzy did her best but couldn't imagine what any of it had to do with selling real estate. After the test, she was interviewed by Mr. Foley, who, luckily enough, had apparently learned the routine from the same seminar as her last interviewer. This time, having gone over the questions with Eloise, Suzy was prepared:

MR. FOLEY: What are you good at, Suzy?

SUZY: Just about anything I decide to do.

MR. FOLEY: What awards have you won?

SUZY: I hate to sound like a braggart, but winning is my hobby.

MR. FOLEY: What are your needs?

SUZY: I'm after money and plenty of it.

MR. FOLEY: Where do you expect to be 5 years from now?

SUZY: My goal is to be "salesperson of the year" and to have at least $100,000 invested—in real estate, of course.

MR. FOLEY: What can you do for our company?

SUZY: I expect to give the company loyalty and diligence, and I will help other people at all times.

This was rattled off in a confident and forthright manner, although at the end Suzy wondered if she hadn't accidentally lapsed into the Boy Scout oath. The broker might well have been increduluous or even nauseous. In fact, Mr. Foley almost broke an arm reaching into his drawer for a contract.

Suzy was never sure whether she'd mastered the wonderful world of forms, tests, and interviews, or whether Mr. Foley had simply observed that she could indeed inhale and exhale admirably well. At any rate, by 2:00 P.M. she had a license and a job and was to be found in the better dress department of a local store, playing havoc with the credit account.

READER'S QUIZ

This is a guaranteed foolproof quiz. All answers are correct. Give yourself a mark of 100, and brag a lot.

1. In my state, the acquisition of a real estate license requires

     _____ a. literacy.
     _____ b. political pull.
     _____ c. a good luck charm.
     _____ d. devout prayer.
     _____ e. other

2. In taking the license examination, the most significant help I got was from

_____ a.   a legal dictionary.
_____ b.   my calculator.
_____ c.   someone else's notes.
_____ d.   tranquilizers.
_____ e.   other

3. As an ego trip, job hunting is on a par with

_____ a.   asking my banker for an unsecured loan.
_____ b.   being pulled over for speeding.
_____ c.   returning a shirt to the laundry.
_____ d.   telling my mother I'm pregnant again.
_____ e.   other

4. The best approach to taking a psychological test might be

_____ a.   to decorate the answer sheet with an attractive geometric pattern.
_____ b.   to think of a successful person and answer the way I think he or she would.
_____ c.   to spill ink globs over dubious answers.
_____ d.   eeny, meeny, miney, mo.
_____ e.   other

5. I chose to join the company I affiliated with because

_____ a.   their office is air-conditioned.
_____ b.   their signs are in my favorite colors.
_____ c.   their broker drives a Lincoln Continential.
_____ d.   nobody else asked me.
_____ e.   other

"Wow! I'm gonna love this," Bitsy enthused.

"I must warn you," Hubert hastened to add, "those who come in late and fail to attend meetings generally don't make effective salespeople. They may find themselves regretfully terminated at an early date."

"Do I smell a rat?" Suzy whispered to Clara.

"Uh hum," Clara nodded in agreement.

Next, the newcomers were briefed on the company's history and structure. Realtor Foley, Hubert explained, had charge of all residential brokerage. Realtor Feinberg was the commercial-investment broker. Realtor Chong was the company treasurer in charge of borrowing, check-writing, and maintaining an eagle-eyed scrutiny over all company expenditures. It was regrettable that the principals weren't on hand to greet them in person; however, Foley was at the country club, Feinberg was attending a seminar, and Chong was at the bank. This, they were to discover, was usually the case.

Hubert showed them around the office and demonstrated the copying machine, although he had to elbow several frenzied agents aside to do so. He introduced them to a bewildering bevy of managers, salespeople, coordinators of this and that, and secretary-clerks. All wore harried expressions and inhabited desks piled high with paperwork and cold coffee. They seemed to have telephones permanently attached to their ears. The total effect was pure chaos—like a frat house at homecoming, or backstage before curtain time.

The day ended on a high note. Hubert gave a sparkling 30-minute motivational talk that sent Suzy home glowing with optimism. She babbled about goals all through dinner.

"It's hard to tell whether you've come from a real estate office or a hockey game," John said indulgently.

The second session of training was less effervescent and definitely more businesslike.

"This is a basic list of things you'll need," Hubert announced, as he passed sheets of paper around. "Cards, forms, blue books, sign riders, car signs, desk name plates, and so on. Just mark the box next to the ones you want to order now."

"Looks like nice stuff, but it's so expensive," Bitsy exclaimed. "Will the company pay for it?"

"Of course we'd be happy to do that if we could," Hubert replied. "But since you're independent contractors . . . "

"You can't. Great cop-out!" Joel cried. "But that also means we don't have to buy it if we don't want to, right Hubert?"

"Well, I can *hardly* see how you could do without any of these items," Hubert replied sternly.

So, with checkbooks in hand, the group lined up in front of the company bookkeeper. Mrs. Niggardly was a hatchet-faced woman with a whiny voice and a perpetually wounded manner. The group anxiety level rose with every click of her calculator.

"Will somebody tell me what this is all about?" Bitsy asked plaintively.

"It's about $140.75," Clara replied tartly.

The cash drain continued as they moved on to the next item of business, membership in the local Board of Realtors® and the multiple-listing service. Hubert dolled out another dose of what Suzy had come to think of as ICP, or independent contractor paradox. He stressed that membership was not required but that the company had grave reservations about affiliating with any agent who wouldn't join these worthy organizations. Suzy duly chose to become a Realtor-Associate®, an MLS member, and another $75 poorer. By now she strongly suspected that the checking account was overdrawn.

Finally the buying spree ended and the group settled down to view a sprightly film entitled "Let's Get Personal." It was all about smoking, drinking, gum chewing (John would have loved that part), language, driving habits, hairdos, clothing, and general appearance. When it was over, Suzy breathed a sigh of relief. It had stopped short of recommending a mouthwash and underarm deodorant. Afterwards Hubert explained that the film presented only suggestions since FFC didn't have a dress code (ICP?). He then reviewed a long list of things an agent must have on hand at all times.

"Do we get a desk to stash all this stuff?" Joel asked.

"Goodness, no. That isn't the way we operate in the real estate business," Hubert replied. FFC has 40 agents using just eight desks. The important things go in a briefcase. You'll need to find a quiet little corner in your home to use as an office—any spot big enough for a desk, file cabinet, and phone will do. Some salespeople outfit the back of their cars as a traveling office."

Suzy went home with her brain buzzing. Obviously the little patent leather purse would have to be replaced by something halfway between an overnight bag and a steamer trunk. Could the pantry be converted to an office? Where, then, would the food go? How many gates and locks would render it safe from vandalous juveniles in search of peanut butter? Maybe the old sedan should be traded in on a nine-passenger station wagon. Since it wasn't likely that John would appreciate any of these schemes, the Soldsines' evening was unusually quiet.

On the third day, Suzy was amused to note that Joel had combed his hair and put on an acceptable shirt. Bitsy, too, had been moved by the previous day's "suggestions" and had abandoned her ruffles for a tailored suit. Suzy had to admit that Bitsy would have looked frivolous and sexy in a straight jacket. Karl and Clara apparently saw no need to change, and Suzy, still in the navy blue, was beginning to wonder if the "outfit" should now more properly be called the "uniform."

The trainees tackled methods for evaluating property. Hubert explained about researching comparables, or recently sold properties that are similar to the one being evaluated. Suzy felt at home with comparables, as she'd covered them in her prelicense class. She was not, however, prepared for an infernal machine called a computer terminal. Suzy instinctively distrusted any mechanism more complex than a nail file. The computer, with its ultra-human intelligence, left her in abject terror. Hubert talked about the computer is if it were his own precocious child. He exerted all his persuasive powers to convince the group that the device was not only fast, infallible, and easy to use, but also essential to the practice of real estate in the modern world.

When they finally got around to working out comparable problems, each trainee got a chance to try out the machine. Karl greeted it as an old friend, Joel as a manageable servant, Bitsy with wonder and awe, and Clara with her sleeves rolled up. Suzy approached the machine with her knees knocking. She expected a hostile reaction and was not disappointed. The terminal digested her input with a series of beeps and boops and responded with the single, telltale line:

None   None   None   None   None

As the training continued, Hubert laid careful groundwork for the all-important task of obtaining listings. Relatives, neighbors, friends, and acquaintances, he insisted, were no longer anything of the sort. They were now potential listings.

"But," he added (Hubert was full of *buts),* "they won't provide enough leads. You have to talk to strangers."

"You mean ring doorbells like the Avon lady?" Bitsy asked with a giggle.

"That's the idea," Hubert replied. "We'll assign each of you a 'farm.' That's a neighborhood where you can become familiar with all the houses and all the people by calling on them."

"Do we have to?" Bitsy queried.

"It isn't difficult. We have nice folks in this community who need our services. It's up to you to let them know those services are available."

At the coffee break, the gang gathered to hash over this new development.

"I don't know," Suzy shook her head, "mother always told me not to talk to strangers."

"Undignified! That's what it is," Karl growled. "I'll get all the listings I need from the men in my old command."

Joel nodded his agreement, "Hey, man. I'm not hung up on the dignity trip. But I intend to specialize in a higher-type of clientele—not Mr. and Mrs. Suburbia."

"Daddy promised to take care of bringing me listings," Bitsy said. No one deigned to ask her who "daddy" might be. (Foley? Feinberg? Chong? The mayor?)

"Well, I'm damned if any stranger's going to intimidate me," Clara said. "Bring on the doorbells!"

Women resist carrying an attache case.

Suzy decided to team up with Clara. The subject of talking to strangers was not to be dismissed without actual practice. Like fledgling recruits in basic training, crawling on their bellies through an obstacle course under fire, the new agents under Hubert's command were taken to a residential neighborhood and set to ringing doorbells. They were fortified by instructions about whistling up the walk, smiling, making the right opening remarks. Most would have preferred a strong belt of bourbon.

Out of 50 homes on their list, there were 20 with no one at home. Another 5 were skipped because of hostile animals. (Hubert wasn't too pleased about that development and was heard to mutter that Bitsy would probably be frightened by a goldfish). In at least 10 other calls they interrupted the homeowners in the midst of some important undertaking. Notable, was the woman who came to the door wearing nothing but a string of pearls—an incident that caused Karl's blood pressure to soar far above the fail-safe level.

As they discussed it later, the trainees had to admit that Hubert was at least partly right. No one had been stabbed, shot, or even punched in the nose. It was indeed true that people enjoy talking about their homes. In fact, "My House" may well be the second most popular topic of conversation in Suburbia, USA. And quite possibly the first in the over-60 age group.

The final weeks of training whizzed by as the class continued to absorb fundamentals. In a whirlwind of lectures, films, cassettes, demonstrations, and role-playing, they took up:

- The listing contract (with horror stories about the dire consequences of failing to properly research the property)

- Telephone technique (and the importance of always answering a question with a question)

- Ad writing (tell them enough but not too much, the truth but not the whole truth)

- Time management (have a daily plan, but don't necessarily stick to it)

- Qualifying the buyer (you have two ears and one mouth—use them in that proportion)

- Showing technique (do *not* point out that the refrigerator is a refrigerator—they already know that)

- Handling objections (which are not really objections at all, but must be dealt with in some fashion beforehand, now, later, or never)

- Eight surefire closing techniques (with no reason given why you need eight if they're so surefire)

- Follow-up (today's buyer is tomorrow's seller)

Hubert saved his favorite topic for last—the various ways to finance the purchase. There were 35 in all, and everyone (except Joel, of course) fell by the wayside long before that number was reached. Suzy had already experienced a cultural conflict in being told to talk to strangers. Didn't mother always describe that as an invitation to unwanted advances? Mother also often said that borrowing money is an intrinsically evil practice. Now Hubert would have Suzy believe that borrowing is a pleasurable and productive pastime—also essential to the nation's economy. She was prepared to believe it but not entirely prepared to cope with such innovations as variable rates, graduated payment plans, and escalation clauses. The finance lecture called for another dose of encouragement via a phone call to good old Eloise.

"Don't be silly, darling," Eloise cried. "There's nothing to it. Just go to the lending institution, grab the doorknob firmly in your right hand, and push. Then ask your favorite loan officer to do all the work."

Reassured, Suzy accepted her diploma from the training course and set forth to commit real estate. On her way home she stopped at a lunch counter for a snack. A pleasant-looking man sat down next to her. He made a casual comment about the weather and flashed a warm smile. Mother's Suzy would have beaten a hasty retreat, but the new Suzy, reprogrammed by friend Hubert, was ready to talk to strangers.

"Hi," she said brightly, "I'm Suzy Soldsine with FFC Realty Company."

"What do you know," he replied. "This must be my lucky day. I was just sitting here thinking about a house I'd like to sell. Maybe we can get together and discuss it."

Surely during 3 solid weeks of basic nitty-gritty, Hubert must have covered what one says in this situation. Probably he'd given them 3, 5, maybe even 10 suitable responses. What she said was:

"You gotta be kidding!"

From that day forward, mother be damned, Suzy was a firm believer in talking to strangers. She sought them out, struck up conversations with them, cultivated them, and on occasion went in vigorous pursuit. To be sure, there was still the chance that a stranger might prove dangerous, but it was more likely to be the other way around.

READER'S QUIZ

This is a guaranteed foolproof quiz. All answers are correct. Give yourself a mark of 100, and brag a lot.

1. The training director of a real estate company is usually selected because of exceptional ability to

   _____ a.   ring doorbells.
   _____ b.   thread the movie projector.
   _____ c.   run the coffee machine.
   _____ d.   justify the company's commission-split policy.
   _____ e.   other

2. My very first week in real estate produced

   _____ a.   a parking ticket.
   _____ b.   a broken heel.
   _____ c.   a splitting headache.
   _____ d.   a marital crisis.
   _____ e.   other

3. The single most important item a salesperson must have on hand at all times is

   _____ a.   change for the pay phone.
   _____ b.   more change for parking meters.
   _____ c.   a spare tire.
   _____ d.   aspirin and Tums.
   _____ e.   other

4. Most of the women in real estate prefer to carry their equipment around in

   _____ a.   a Gucci bag.
   _____ b.   a carpetbag.
   _____ c.   a shopping bag.
   _____ d.   a garbage bag.
   _____ e.   other

5. In evaluating residential properties, new agents generally resort to

   _____ a.   asking the computer.
   _____ b.   asking an old agent for help.
   _____ c.   asking the sellers what they think.
   _____ d.   asking for a leave of absence.
   _____ e.   other

4
Monday Morning Motivation

In real estate, as in most other businesses, the workweek begins at a depressingly early hour on Monday morning. There, however, all similarities end. Most working people are devout, dues-paying members of the Thank-God-It's-Friday Club. They finish up on Friday afternoon and have 2 glorious days to dally before returning to the fray on Monday morning. In real estate, the workweek ends on Sunday night and rarely in time for 8 hours' sleep.

Suzy spent her first Sunday evening in the business with her lunch-counter acquaintance, Mr. Golden. With no chance to research the property, she hadn't the faintest idea of its market value. In fact, she wasn't even sure she could find the place. Literally trembling with fear, Suzy stuffed the contract forms into one of John's old briefcases. Also included were aspirins, a compass, extra pantyhose, and a moth-eaten rabbit's foot Mike had been carrying around since the fourth grade.

As she fumbled with the catches, Suzy was unable to recall more than 2 percent of what Hubert had taught her about the listing presentation. But she did manage to motivate herself out of the house and into the car by making quick calculations of commissions to be earned at various prices . . . and by fervent prayer. Said prayer was answered—or maybe it was the rabbit's foot—Mr. Golden turned out to be a mortgage lender. He knew all the things that Suzy didn't know and quite possibly a lot that she'd never know. Mr. Golden named his price, filled out his own contract, and signed it with no questions asked.

The next morning, the FFC week began with the usual Monday morning sales meeting for all the associates. Naturally, they were expected to show up on time and fired up with energy for the week ahead. Suzy certainly was. As for the rest of the staff, the minds may have been willing, but the bodies were obviously weak. No doubt the majority were still victims of habits learned in other fields of endeavor, where one starts the week in the pits, gradually elevates to the tolerable level by Wednesday, and does not quite achieve enthusiasm before 5:00 P.M. on Friday. The manager in charge of motivating this group had a challenge about equal to that of a temperance worker in a pub on St. Patrick's Day.

"Sell, sell, sell!"

Forty-six licenses were displayed handsomely on the office wall. The sales meeting was supposed to bring all of the bearers together; however, Suzy counted only 23 bodies present. A few of the absentees may well have had valid excuses, since they did appear at later meetings. The others were simply disinclined to attend meetings, sufficiently versed in the independent contractor concept to believe that they didn't have to, and/or were productive enough to get away with it. At least 10 of the names on the wall never did show up at the office in any way, shape, or form. "Have they retired, absconded, or just passed away?" Suzy wondered. No one seemed to know or care.

The meeting was conducted by the sales manager, whom everyone called "Buster." Buster had a round, ruddy face, a shock of unruly hair, and a short, wiry frame that exuded nervous energy. Physically he could have been Hubert's twin, and he spoke in the same staccato. But, while Hubert overflowed with enthusiasm, Buster had the air of a man who rarely enjoys a good night's sleep, never has time to jog, and usually forgets to take his multiple vitamins. Buster apologized for starting the meeting late. There had been an urgent, 20-minute conversation with an irate client. This, Suzy was to discover, is how a manager's Monday morning usually begins. Also Tuesday, Wednesday, Thursday, and Friday.

While waiting, the agents had attacked the coffee machine and had demonstrated a formidable capacity for consumption of that life-breathing beverage. They had also engaged in shoptalk, swapping tales about unrealistic sellers, cantankerous buyers, difficult tenants, heartless lenders, and inefficient escrow officers. Some of the language was not even comprehensible to Suzy. While she had mastered legal terminology, she had yet to learn that a "fizz-bo" is a for sale by owner, a "vroom" is a variable rate mortgage, and that "courtesy to brokers" has little to do with being polite.

Finally, the meeting began. Buster asked the agents to present their new listings. Suzy's hand was the first to go up. Though Mr. Golden's house was small and rather run-of-the-mill, she described it to her cohorts as a sort of cross between the Taj Mahal and the Palace at Versailles. Both Buster and Hubert were inordinately pleased with her achievement and took turns lavishing praise on her.

Now, praise is a heady experience for an erstwhile homemaker accustomed to being rewarded for a gourmet meal with a few satisfied grunts and a mountain of dirty dishes. Suzy reveled in her moment of glory, her smile broadening and her head rising higher with each commendation. The bubble burst abruptly, though, when Buster began to call on the other agents. Harry was a likable, grey-haired man, a fatherly figure who chewed an unlit pipe and said very little. That morning, he reported three new listings and two sales. Next came Helga, a wonder woman, who offhandedly announced five new listings and three sales as if that were just an average week's work. These accomplishments occasioned praise in even greater measures than Suzy had received, including bonus checks and a 30-second appearance by Mr. Foley, who gave Helga a hug.

The agents who had no new listings provided an interesting variety of excuses. Some seemed to accept their slumps quite cheerfully, but a few dour souls were heard to say they were thinking of changing companies.

"Obviously, Harry and Helga are getting all the good leads," groused one.

"And the best floor time, too," agreed another.

Overhearing that last remark, Buster scowled. "I thought we'd agreed to bury that phrase. 'Floor time' implies that the company *requires* you to spend time in the office. 'Opportunity time,' as you well know, is entirely optional. I'll pass the sign-up sheet right now."

"What if nobody signs?" Suzy asked innocently.

"We have to have an agent on hand at all times to take care of any client who calls or drops in," Buster replied.

"It's to your advantage," Hubert added. "If you're the one on duty, the client is yours."

"Yea, unless they ask for somebody else," said one of the disgruntled agents. "I'm damned if I like taking messages for other people and waiting for lightning to strike."

"Take a lot if you can, Suzy," Harry advised. "It's good experience, and it does pay off once in awhile."

By the time the sheet got around to Suzy, only Wednesday morning was open. She started to write in her name just as Helga, who'd left the room to take a phone call, reentered. Helga grabbed the sheet from Suzy and flew into a rage.

"Buster, this idiot is signing up for *my time*!" she shrieked. "If you let this happen, I'll . . . "

"Now Helga, I'm sure Suzy didn't realize you always have Wednesdays," he said wearily.

"Should have warned you," Harry chuckled. "Taking Helga's time is as risky as taking cubs from a dyspeptic mother bear."

The novices, eager for opportunity time, found none to be had. "You'll get your chance when others call in for replacements," Buster assured them.

The sales meeting then progressed to another standard item, the company's advertising policy. Helga had been denied a special picture ad on one of her higher-priced listings and was properly irate. By routine, such requests were always submitted to Mrs. Niggardly, who invariably said she'd have to ask Mr. Chong. Mr. Chong almost always said no. On rare occasions he said *"Hell, no!"*

At first, Buster tried to justify the company's position, but he remained a lonely minority of one. Finally, he agreed to talk to Mr.

Chong about a more liberal advertising budget. The betting was that this would be a *"Hell, no!"* occasion.

With an extraordinarily poor sense of timing, Buster then read a stern note from Mr. Chong, who wished to discourage the agents' excessive use of the copying machine, to recommend reheating yesterday's coffee before making a new pot, and to extoll the virtues of short pencils.

Finally, after a few brief announcements about meetings, seminars, and loan policy changes, Hubert was called upon to give an inspirational talk. He delivered an abbreviated version of the speech that had fired Suzy's imagination during the training course. However, she didn't find it quite so stimulating the second time around. Judging from the looks, attitudes, and hasty departures of the seasoned agents, they may have heard it more than twice.

After the sales meeting, most of the group piled into cars to "caravan" the new listings. Suzy hadn't realized she'd be expected to show Mr. Golden's house. Fortunately, it was vacant and she had the key. However, as the group raced through one house after another, she felt increasingly uneasy. The salespeople attacked each other's properties without mercy, noting every flaw. In almost every case, they concluded that the listing was overpriced and would be hard to sell. Harry noticed her discomfort and explained the psychology of this routine.

"When the listing's a dog, you'll hear only some mild nit-picking. A really nice house brings out the big guns."

"But why?" Suzy queried. "Don't we sell a house on its good points?"

"They want to discourage anyone else from showing it before they can call their own prospective buyers."

"Helga really pulled that last one to pieces; she must have a hot prospect," Suzy observed.

Harry chuckled, "When an agent can't find one single redeeming feature—well, to me that says she wants to buy it herself."

Suzy was glad Harry had straightened this out before they got to Mr. Golden's house. No one mentioned any resemblance to the Taj Mahal. Suzy herself was dismayed to discover that the house had shrunk overnight. Surely the broken porch step and the peeling wallpaper in the kitchen hadn't been there yesterday! The salespeople made their snide remarks, but two of them asked for appointments to show.

"Good work," Buster said. "Nice little house and listed at a salable price."

Suzy thanked Buster and silently blessed Mr. Golden.

"Get an ad in on this right away," Buster continued. "And plan to hold it open Sunday afternoon."

After the caravan, the agents returned to the office, where there was a mad scramble to use the facilities. Waiting her turn, Suzy noted that, in spite of 2 hours on the road preceded by gallons of coffee, Helga made six phone calls before visiting the rest room. At one point she was carrying on two conversations simultaneously with an instrument pressed to each ear. Suzy wondered if "being like Helga" could be considered a valid goal. On reflection, she decided that, though her ears might prove equal to the task, her bladder would never make it.

Hubert suggested that the five trainees put their heads together to compose Suzy's first ad. He reminded them that the most important part of the ad is the heading. It should be very brief, a distilled essence of the property's most salable feature, and couched in emotional rather than factual terms.

"Remember," he said as they departed to exercise their creative talents over hamburgers, "people buy houses emotionally."

Karl may or may not have remembered this point when he opened the discussion. "I have the heading for you, he announced—"City Sewer."

"Oh, yuk!" Bitsy cried.

Suzy was a bit more diplomatic. "It's a good thought, Karl. But it misses on the emotional appeal."

"Sewage is a most important consideration," Karl insisted. "Any buyer who's had my experiences with septic tanks can relate to it, I promise you."

"But it's a perfect little house for a first-time buyer. They don't know anything about sewers or septic tanks," Clara argued.

"Then we have a moral obligation to educate them," Karl replied staunchly.

Predictably, none of the others saw the sewage system as an emotionally appealing feature, nor were they prepared to educate the public on this point.

"Suzy," Clara said thoughtfully, "didn't Hubert say that the seller's own motivation when he bought the house would give us a clue? Why did Mr. Golden buy it?"

"He said he picked it up at a foreclosure sale 2 years ago—saw a chance to make a profit. If you want to translate that into emotion, I guess you'd have to call it greed."

This prompted Joel to whip out his H-P calculator, from which he extracted a dizzying array of numbers. As he punched the buttons, Joel mumbled incoherently about internal rates of return adjusted for an annual inflation rate of 11.2 percent over 5-, 10-, and 15-year holding periods. Although Joel was obviously enjoying the exercise, Suzy couldn't see "Astronomical Profit Potential" as the proper heading for her little house. The rest of the group found it about as exciting as Karl's "City Sewer" entry.

At this point, Suzy felt their efforts would benefit from the ultra-feminine perspective, so she asked Bitsy what had impressed her about the house.

"Actually, I wasn't all that crazy about it, Bitsy giggled. "But I did turn on to the pink and white color scheme in the master bedroom and bath . . . and those cute little flowered tiles.

"Sexy Bedroom and Bath" was briefly considered and quickly discarded.

"I'm afraid it would attract the wrong class of people," Suzy said.

"And for all the wrong reasons," Clara added.

They finally settled for "Inexpensive," although Joel claimed to have counted 41 "Inexpensives" in the previous day's paper. After all, the classified ad section is the final resting place of shopworn phrases and utter cliches. And none of them had ever claimed to be poet laureates. One thing they did learn and learn well—ad writing is a loathsome task.

On the way back to the office, the word "Shipshape" popped into Suzy's mind. She wound up rewriting the whole thing and was justifiably pleased with the end result. She bounced it off Harry, who pronounced it inspired. Then, she turned the copy in to Mrs. Niggardly. The bookkeeper didn't bother to read it, but glanced at it briefly and whined to Suzy that it was far too long and much too late. The ad did, in fact, appear in the newspaper on the following Sunday; however, it was considerably abbreviated from the masterpiece Suzy had submitted.

During the balance of Suzy's first week in real estate, she addressed 200 little cards to friends and acquaintances, announcing her new career and soliciting their business. She waited for the phone to ring and learned another of life's painful truths—phones never ring when you want them to. Suzy had calculated that she could earn $1,320 if she could find a buyer for her listing. She entertained some delicious thoughts about how to spend the money and looked forward eagerly to her Sunday open house. As it happened, Helga sold the house on Friday night.

The offer was full price, and Mr. Golden promptly accepted it. Suzy earned $480. Helga earned $840, which caused Suzy to wonder whose interests Hubert had at heart when he laid so much emphasis on the importance of listings. Still, Mr. Golden was pleased. John would be pleased, too. He'd better be. Her total of $480 was more than she'd been able to amass in 4 full years as chairman of the Girl Scout cookie drive.

READER'S QUIZ

This is a guaranteed foolproof quiz. All answers are correct. Give your-self a mark of 100, and brag a lot.

1.   Real estate agents come to the weekly sales meeting

_____ a.   late.
_____ b.   reluctantly.
_____ c.   as long as the coffee is free.
_____ d.   because they have nothing better to do.
_____ e.   other

2.   The top salesperson in an office is usually

_____ a.   the luckiest.
_____ b.   the broker's pet.
_____ c.   the most neurotic.
_____ d.   the least popular.
_____ e.   other

3.   Agents welcome "opportunity time" because it affords them a chance to

_____ a.   tie up the phone lines.
_____ b.   clean out their desks.
_____ c.   work a crossword puzzle.
_____ d.   make out with a secretary.
_____ e.   other

4.   To salespeople, the job of composing classified ads is on a par with

_____ a.   writing the Great American Novel.
_____ b.   answering a chain letter.
_____ c.   making out an income tax return.
_____ d.   writing a letter to the gas company's computer.
_____ e.   other

5.   When I told my spouse about my first commission, he/she

_____ a.   expressed disbelief.
_____ b.   applied for early retirement.
_____ c.   bought an oil well.
_____ d.   went on a bender.
_____ e.   other

5
Never Underestimate the Power

As Mr. Golden's property was no longer available, Suzy felt sure her open house would be canceled. She was even entertaining some unsalespersonlike thoughts about a leisurely Sunday with the family when Buster burst that bubble with the flat-out statement that it was too late to cancel the ad.

"Besides," he added, "houses that have already been sold are the very best kind to hold open."

"And they say women don't make any sense," Suzy was thinking.

"We don't have the house open just because we want to sell it," Buster went on.

"You could have fooled me," Suzy muttered.

"What you're after, my dear, is buyer prospects," he explained. "When they come to see a property and discover that someone else has beaten them to it, they develop that all-important sense of urgency. Show them something else that suits their purposes, and they'll grab it."

"Yes, but what else is there to show them?" Suzy asked, feeling somewhat dimwitted.

"You'll have to make a 'switch list,'" said Buster, looking a trifle annoyed.

"A what?"

"Go through the MLS book. Pick out the current listings that are similar to your house—same size, price, general location. It'll take 5 minutes if you use the computer."

Switch lists. Now that was something Suzy could relate to. Like using cornflakes in the cookie batter when you're out of Rice Crispies. Or pinning a ripped hem with cellophane tape. Homemakers are generally out of something, so switch lists become part of their natural survival instinct.

Using the computer, however, was definitely treading into alien territory. Luckily, Suzy spied Joel leaning against the coffee machine, evidently waiting for his brilliance to be discovered. She used Joel, who used the computer, and the switch list was in hand in no time. Suzy congratulated herself. Her feminine ingenuity obviously translated into an instinctive flare for the demanding work of real estate.

Hubert had taught the new agents to prepare for an open house as if preparing for a party in their own home. Suzy had always loved playing hostess and threw herself into the role with great gusto. This usually produced some grumbling from John, who never could understand why a household must be disrupted for days in advance in order to produce a few hours of conviviality. In this case, she had only one day to prepare, and the grumbling was more pronounced as Suzy sped off to scrub Mr. Golden's house, leaving John to scrub their own.

By the appointed hour, the house was ready to be shown. There were fresh flowers in the living room and soft drinks in the refrigerator. Suzy, dressed in something long and flowing, was poised at the front door— smile on her face, guest book in hand, and contract forms conveniently nearby. One hour later, the first couple arrived, a middle-aged pair who looked as if they had been discussing the gas crisis.

"Hi there. Please come on in," Suzy said brightly. "My name is Suzy Soldsine, and you are . . . ?"

Hubert had drilled them in this opener, vowing it would never fail to produce the desired name. Hubert was wrong. Mr. and Mrs. Sourpuss failed to respond.

"Would you care to sign our guest book?" Suzy asked.

"No," said Mr. Sourpuss, tossing the response over his shoulder and dismissing Suzy as if her sole function had been to open the door for him. (Another X for Hubert.)

The Sourpusses trotted through the house at a pace just under a dead run, their muttered comments inaudible and, judging from their expressions, totally unfavorable. Racing after them, Suzy decided that this was certainly the time to wheel out the good old "sense of urgency." She managed to trap them in the kitchen and catching her breath, said:

"I think I should tell you that this house was sold the day before yesterday. But we do have others. . . ."

"Well, I never!" said Mrs. Sourpuss testily. "Why in the world are we wasting our time here, I'd like to know?" And with that, they exited in a huff. So much for the sense of urgency.

Shortly after this disquieting episode, the next party arrived—a young woman accompanied by three small, grubby children and a seemingly endless supply of chocolate, licorice, and bubble gum. Suzy performed a bit better this time. She did manage to get a name and address in the pristine guest book. She also learned that Mrs. Longacre wasn't interested in buying a home, but just liked looking. It kept the children occupied and out of the reach of a father who was inclined to violence when his Sunday afternoon television was interrupted. For her efforts, Suzy earned the privilege of rehanging a curtain, repotting a plant, picking up a basketful of trash, and scrubbing sticky fingerprints off practically everything after the Longacres' leisurely departure.

Another lull carried her through to closing time. Just as Suzy was locking up, a third prospect arrived, a couple in their middle 30s. Feeling that John's morning grumbling might turn into something more acute if he had to start supper, Suzy almost wished that the new arrivals would disappear. Instead, they plopped themselves down in comfortable chairs and obligingly informed her that they were Mr. and Mrs. Green and that they owned an accounting firm. The Greens were looking for a home within a short distance of their office.

"We've been through 11 houses this afternoon, and I'm dead beat," Mrs. Green added. "But this looks like a definite possiblity."

It hardly seemed the appropriate moment to inform the poor lady that the house was no longer available, but Suzy dutifully turned on her sold-but-we-have-others speech. Encouraged when the Greens didn't immediately bolt for the door, she threw in another of Hubert's surefire winners—the "feel, felt, found" routine.

"I know exactly how you *feel*. House hunting is really an exhausting experience. I've been there a time or two myself, and I've always *felt* the same way. However, we've *found* that listings don't last very long in this active market. You have to keep looking. Be ready to jump when the right thing turns up. Perhaps I can help by showing you a few other properties that are similar to this one and might suit your needs."

The Greens were either impressed or too tired to argue. They weren't up for any more viewing that afternoon, but Suzy did obtain an appointment to show them houses on the following day. Only after they'd left did she realize that she'd neglected to ask what they'd already seen.

On the whole, though, Suzy felt she'd done rather well. She had a buyer prospect who might even be harboring a latent sense of urgency. Moreover, not once in the entire afternoon had she succumbed to the temptation to point out that the refrigerator was a refrigerator. She felt decidedly professional.

On Monday, Suzy showed three houses to the Greens, having—per Hubert's instructions—done her homework first. She had picked up keys, viewed the homes herself, and made copious notes.

As Suzy and her prospects stepped into the entrance hall of the first house, it became immediately apparent that the Greens were experienced house hunters and extremely detailed in their approach. They pulled out tape measures and proceeded to analyze:

- how far Mrs. G. would have to walk from the car to the kitchen with the groceries

- whether the hall closet could accommodate the extra leaves for the dining room table

- if there was suitable wall space in the living room for a large breakfront

- how convenient was the route for conveying dirty clothes from the bedrooms to the washing machine

- if the refrigerator could comfortably hold gallon jugs of milk and the oven embrace a 20-pound turkey

And much more of the same. This house was found to be defective in a number of areas: the top shelves of the kitchen cupboards were one-half inch beyond Mrs. G's reach; a semi-sleepwalker would have to pass an open stairway enroute from bedroom to bathroom; moreover, said bathroom lacked storage space for a 6-months' supply of toilet tissue.

It all made perfect sense to Suzy. Working with the Greens reaffirmed her conviction that residential selling is woman's work. Men tend to look at the whole house—a major asset with predictable monthly upkeep costs and occasional unpredictable expenses. Women see the house as an environment. It's the setting within which they perform the infinitely varied tasks of homemaking. The layout of the house and the quality of the equipment have everything to do with making the homemaker's job manageable or miserable. In other words, an ill-placed step between the kitchen and the garage is no minor matter to a homemaker. It will annoy her approximately 5 times a day, 115 times a month, or 1,835 times a year.

While Suzy was entirely in tune with the Greens' concerns, she was getting the uncomfortable feeling that no house on Earth (much less in their price bracket) could possibly measure up. For the first time and for many times to come, she despaired that most of the world's architects and designers are men. Tall men, probably, and almost certainly bachelors.

"Whoever heard of a bathroom without a single square inch of storage space?" Mrs. Green exclaimed with annoyance.

Suzy nodded in sympathy. "I guess it goes along with shelves you can't reach, children's clothes you can't machine wash, and cups you can't drink out of without dribbling down your chin."

"Right," agreed Mrs. G., warming to the topic. "And don't forget about hotdogs."

"What about hotdogs?" Mr. G. asked, as if he thought he had missed something.

The women replied in unison, "They come 10 to a pack. Hotdog rolls come eight to a pack."

This evidently gave Mr. G. food for deep thought becuase he remained silent throughout the inspections of houses 2 and 3. Although, predictably, neither was perfect, house 2 did emerge as the best of the three. The Greens really liked the house. But it was listed at $10,000 above their indicated comfort zone. Suzy could clearly remember Hubert saying not once but repeatedly: "Remember, price is never really a valid objection. If they find the house they want, they'll find a way to pay for it."

Obviously, Hubert had never sold houses to accountants. Suzy reached into her bag for an offer form; the Greens packed away their tape measures and pulled out their programmed calculators. An hour of playing with numbers and they were just warming up. Mr. Green was beginning to have a security crisis about getting it all home and plugging into his tabletop computer.

Suzy knew better than to settle for a buyer's decision to "think it over overnight." But she'd never been taught how to handle a client who wants to calculate all night. Finally, they arranged to meet the next day and write up an offer.

It was a heady experience. Two weeks in the business—not even that—and she'd racked up two transactions totaling more than $1,000 in commissions. Suzy sang all the way home and burst in the door shouting, "John, the Greens are going to buy! Now I can have my piano!"

"Whoa, there, Suzy," John replied anxiously. "You've had a couple of good weeks and that's great. But we haven't seen the first dollar yet. There might just be some bad times along with the good ones. Let's not spend the loot before you've set a track record."

"I don't intend to pay cash for it," Suzy explained. "They have a monthly payment plan. That's exactly the motivation I need. Buster says motivation is the key to success, and monthly payments are very motivational."

John frowned. "I'll just bet Buster says that," he said picking up the evening paper with a gesture calculated to end the conversation.

Suzy was just as pleased to let the matter drop. Years of marriage, and a number of painful episodes, had taught her that men and women simply practice different theories of money management. The male is pragmatic; he'll spend only what he can count on, tailoring his expenses to meet his earnings, with a bit put aside for the proverbial rainy day. No doubt it's a holdover from primitive times when he had to go forth and hunt food for his family. The male actually considers the possiblity of coming up empty-handed. In a situation where his next month's earnings are a question mark, he is basically insecure.

Like most women she knew, Suzy had a more creative approach. She decided what she wanted to spend first, then she worked out ways of making it possible. The female has an innately positive attitude about her chances of wheedling money out of dear old dad, darling husband, or kind fate. Consequently, the feminine approach is ideally suited to the flexibility of commission earnings—another reason, Suzy reflected with satisfaction, why women go so well with real estate, and vice versa.

The positive thinking carried through to the next morning's sales meeting, where Suzy casually announced that she'd have to skip the caravan because of an appointment to write an offer. Her training class buddies were duly impressed, none of them as yet having put pen to paper. The happy balloon popped at the end of the meeting when Suzy picked up a message that the Greens had canceled. After 24 hours of absolute agony, she finally reached them; they had been cruising around and had uncovered three more houses they wanted to see. So, Suzy dug in her heels and showed houses 4, 5, and 6. In subsequent days, she also showed houses 7 through 17. The tape measures, the calculators, and Suzy's patience were wearing thin.

With a positively fairy-godmotherish sense of timing, Eloise popped in and invited Suzy to lunch. While Eloise poured wine, Suzy poured out her tale of woe.

"Sounds like you just haven't generated any sense of urgency," said Eloise thoughtfully.

"Damn your silly sense of urgency," Suzy exclaimed, slamming her glass down and spilling wine on the tablecloth. "Buster said they'd already be feeling that. The first house I showed them was sold before they got there. I think accountants are immune to urgency."

"You're probably right. Engineers, too, by the way. I avoid them like the plague. They're invariably ectomorphs."

"What in the world is an ectomorph?" Suzy asked.

"A physical type," Eloise explained. "Tall and thin, totally brain-oriented. Most people buy homes because of an emotional response. But ectomorphs just aren't emotional. Am I right? Are the Greens ectomorphs?"

"Come to think of it, they're both tall and painfully thin."

"Aha. There you are, then—that's the problem."

"Marvelous," said Suzy, exasperated. "We've defined the problem. But what in the world do I do about it?"

"I have a feeling you won't like my answer, Suzy. I'd walk away from the whole situation. Devote my time to more promising prospects. The alternative is to show 65 more houses, at which point they'll decide to give up on buying, get a divorce, or join a nomadic desert tribe. One way or another, your time's down the drain."

"Well," said Suzy hesitantly, "I do see your point. It just happens I don't have any other prospects. Besides, Mr. Green keeps saying they *have* to buy because they sold a house last year. Something to do with capital gains taxes."

"M'Gawd," Eloise exclaimed with a jerk that almost sent her chair over backwards. "Why didn't you say so? How long ago did they sell?"

"About 15 months ago, I think. Meanwhile, they're renting."

Eloise chortled with glee. "Hallelujah, baby. You've got it made. They have to buy and close within 18 months in order to defer paying the capital gains tax. Remember now, it takes 4 to 6 weeks to close. They're skating right up to the deadline. That's what I call urgency—the kind accountants can feel right down to the marrow of their ever-lovin' ectomorphic bones. Hang in there, Suzy. An accountant would move into just about anything to avoid paying taxes."

Eloise was right, as usual. Suzy hung in there and showed houses 18 through 24. Then she sat the Greens down and informed them that the time for decision was at hand if they wanted to escape the tax. They were galvanized into action. Within minutes they decided on house 2, still their first choice and, luckily, still available. Just as Hubert had predicted, the price objection evaporated like a teardrop in a desert gale.

Suzy wasn't nervous about writing her first offer. Not, that is, until she got to the very first line, wherein she had to enter the buyers' names. Although she'd been going steady with the Greens for what seemed like a lifetime, she couldn't remember Mr. G's first name. Cleverly, she asked him how he wanted it spelled and was appropriately embarrassed when he answered R-O-B-E-R-T. The fact is, she probably couldn't have brought her own name to mind without consulting her driver's license.

Buster was later to note that the contract contained a number of glaring errors, but at least it was duly written and signed, and accompanied by a check for $1,000 which Suzy tucked into her pocketbook. She fairly flew back to the office to deliver the offer to Buster for presentation to the seller. (It happened that house 2 was Buster's own listing.)

Excitement turned to sheer panic when she reached the office, pulled out the offer, looked for the check, and came up empty. Suzy turned out the contents of her bag on a desk top and pawed frantically through:

- a wallet
- two checkbooks
- a make-up case
- six tired Kleenex tissues
- four department store receipts
- a telephone bill (thought to have been paid)
- three obsolete grocery lists
- Joey's cafeteria card (long since missing)
- three ads for pianos
- a birthday card addressed to her sister that should have been mailed last month
- a how-to booklet on transcendental meditation
- cough drops, mostly out of the box and decidedly sticky
- and no check

"What do you mean you lost the @*&$ deposit check?"

"There, there, dear . . . nothing to cry about . . . we'll find it."

Panic turned to sheer terror as she recalled the chewing-out Harry had received the previous week for losing a contract.

As she heard Buster's baritone approaching in the hall, Suzy did the only thing a woman can realistically do under the circumstances: she burst into tears. Buster put his arm around her, loaned her his handkerchief, and did the only thing a man can realistically do under the circumstances: he pulled a bottle from his bottom drawer and poured a couple of stiff shots. Thus reassured, Suzy returned to the contents of her pocketbook. She did find the check, coated with cough drop stickum and firmly adhered to the inner cover of her checkbook.

The offer was quickly accepted. Suzy felt fantastic. She had now taken a listing that sold, made a sale, earned a dizzying sum of money in a short span of time, and felt well launched on her career. On the way home, she stopped to order her piano.

READER'S QUIZ

This is a guaranteed foolproof quiz. All answers are correct. Give yourself a mark of 100, and brag a lot.

1. An open house in the real estate business is

    _____ a.   more reliable than washing my car for bringing on rain, sleet, or snow.

    _____ b.   like a party—the one I gave for which my husband forgot to mail the invitations.

    _____ c.   a pleasant way to spend a Sunday afternoon, given a good book to read or tv to watch.

    _____ d.   a great way to meet people, some of whom I'd have preferred not to have met.

    _____ e.   other

2. John Q. Homebuyer prefers to be shown houses by a woman because

    _____ a.   a woman knows a kitchen when she sees one and will obligingly point it out.

    _____ b.   with a woman in charge of the tour, he's assured of frequent potty stops.

    _____ c.   a woman is a superior negotiator, having sharpened her skills by arguing with the telephone company's computer.

    _____ d.   John Q. likes women.

    _____ e.   other

3. A sense of urgency is the feeling I get when

    _____ a.   I reach the rest room in the nick of time only to find
                pay stalls and I have no change.
    _____ b.   I am 5 miles from my 11:00 A.M. appointment and it is
                now 11:20.
    _____ c.   I am 3 miles from my 11:00 A.M. appointment; it is now
                11:40, and I have just run out of gas on the freeway.
    _____ d.   I'm about to get up to make a luncheon speech and
                discover that one false eyelash has descended to a posi-
                tion just over my nose.
    _____ e.   other

4. Regarding the differences between men and women, one might say

    _____ a.   women hate to see money wasted—so they put it to
                immediate good use.
    _____ b.   women are more even tempered—sometimes even worse,
                sometimes even better.
    _____ c.   women are more in tune with marketing—they've been
                advertising their wares since Eve.
    _____ d.   hooray!
    _____ e.   other

5. A woman feels comfortable with making switch lists because of
    early training that may have begun when

    _____ a.   her father ran off with a belly dancer.
    _____ b.   her date for the prom got the measles.
    _____ c.   she became too tall to wear her sister's clothes.
    _____ d.   her fiance left her at the church.
    _____ e.   other

6
Why Can't a "Person" Be More Like a Man?

It would be unfair to imply that Suzy's fantastic start established a pattern that was to continue throughout her career. It would also be ridiculous. The real estate business knows no pattern unless it be that of unending change. No 2 days are ever alike. Every property, every client, every buyer, every seller, and every situation is unique. Around each corner lurks the possibility of potential profit—and potential problems. Some mornings the agent wakes up singing "Good morning, God." On others, the refrain is "Good God, it's morning."

The sales staff at FFC were variously impressed by Suzy's jackrabbit start.

"Had her picked for a winner from day one," said Harry.

"The little lady has what it takes," Buster observed. The other successful agents agreed.

"Dumb luck if you ask me," said the losers.

Suzy herself was humbly inclined to share the latter view. She became even more so inclined when the subsequent weeks produced a big fat goose egg. Her first two transactions had closed smoothly, and the first two payments on the piano had been made promptly. But by the time Suzy had moved into the third month of her new career, she was beginning to wonder if her first listing and first sale might also be her last. Suzy had slid into her first slump.

It was some kind of cold comfort to note that all of the salespeople experienced similar ups and downs. Even Helga had a bad month, mainly because she spent it confined to a hospital bed, treating her hard-earned ulcer. Ever the trouper, though, Helga had an extra phone line installed by her bedside and managed to stay in touch.

Buster, too, disappeared from the scene for 3 weeks, apparently enjoying his annual nervous breakdown. Buster's retreat was a mountain cabin, 9 miles from paved road and 14 miles from the nearest model of Alexander Graham Bell's infernal invention.

"A slump," said Hubert ponderously, when Suzy consulted him about her problem, "is what happens when you forget to do the things you were doing when you were successful."

"I wasn't successful long enough to find out what I was doing," Suzy argued to herself.

"Call all of your old clients," Hubert suggested.

"I've already called them both four times," Suzy replied. "Mr. Golden's beginning to wonder about my intentions."

"Think about how you got your last listing, and try the same routine again," was another pearl.

Suzy haunted the lunch counter and talked to strangers. One didn't speak English, three were fellow real estate salespeople, two propositioned her, and one enterprising fellow left her stuck with the check. So much for help from experts.

While Suzy's career was temporarily stalled, she watched her training classmates progress in various directions. Karl decided that selling was not to his liking. The rest of the staff were somewhat surprised, as no one could recall him having tried it. He was rarely seen in the office anymore and explained that he was busy studying for his broker's exam, having determined that management was his proper niche. There was no evidence that anyone else shared this conclusion, but all wished him well.

Joel underwent an amazing metamorphosis. Day by day his locks grew shorter and his clothes more conservative. Finally, he emerged in a three-piece, pin-striped suit, looking for all the world like a banker. Suzy still wondered how his talents would ever be discovered, since he spent the whole day leaning on either the coffee machine or the computer. Strangely enough, that is exactly what happened. Joel was discovered by none other than Mr. Feinberg, whose assistant and understudy he became. Rumor had it that Mr. Feinberg was working on something really big, a rumor, Suzy learned, that had been circulating for several years. Even so, Joel was ecstatic in his new role, playing midwife while the computer gave birth to long and complicated cashflow projections. It wasn't that he stopped talking to the residential sales staff, but as time went by, they understood less and less of what he said.

Bitsy got her big break while showing houses to one of the town's wealthiest industrialists. The client was over 70 and hard of hearing, but Bitsy had a grand time taking him around. Just how many houses they looked at was never quite clear. The client didn't buy one. Still, it would be inaccurate to imply that no sale resulted. After a brief trip to Las Vegas, Bitsy returned to town as Mrs. Industrialist. These days, Bitsy didn't need to work and didn't have the time anyway. But she did drop in occasionally to show off her latest purchases. Success comes in many guises.

Clara was the only one who religiously practiced what they had learned in basic training. A confirmed early riser, self-starter, and daily planner, she made her morning quota of cold telephone calls, then marched forth to ring doorbells in the afternoon. No Fuller Brush person, Avon person, or Seventh-Day Adventist could match her. When Clara had a total of five listings, the other agents began to wonder if "going by the book" might indeed have merit. It looked like a lot of work though, but definitely something to try when all else failed. So Clara plugged on, while the others continued sharpening pencils, shuffling file cards, and waiting for the phone to ring.

Her classmates were moving forward. But none of their successes suggested a solution to Suzy's predicament. She knew she shouldn't follow Karl, couldn't follow Joel, and certainly wouldn't follow Bitsy. That left Clara's plan, which remained for the moment in the last-resort category. In all honesty, the thought of ringing doorbells inspired Suzy with a feverish compulsion to sharpen pencils and shuffle file cards.

John endured Suzy's slump with characteristic patience. He was a veritable encyclopedia of helpful suggestions.

"Hate to see you so depressed, honey," he sympathized. "Even the kids have noticed."

"I know," she replied, "but I'll work it out. It's just that everything was so super teriffic. Then all of a sudden nothing but strikeouts."

"Maybe you shouldn't have tackled it," he said tenderly. "There's a lot of pressure in sales. I'm not entirely convinced women are cut out for that. You girls are always on top of the world or down in the dumps. No talent for staying on an even keel."

"Well, I have tackled it, and I don't intend to quit . . ."

"Hey, I'm not suggesting you quit—just pointing out the options. Remember how gung ho you and Marjorie were to open a boutique? Now, I gather, she's given all that up. Happy to be a housewife again."

"Oh, sure. She's pregnant again—expecting twins, as a matter of fact. Hurray for Marjorie. John, I'm not in the market for babies nor for your damned philosophy. If you want to help, find me a client."

"Maybe you should ask for more floor time," he suggested. "Seems like a pretty good way to pick up leads."

Suzy frowned. "Floor time is a bore, John. All you do is take messages for other people. Most of the time they complain about how you took the message. When the phone isn't ringing, you get to help Mr. Chong count pencil stubs."

"FFC has a great location," John mused. "Don't tell me customers don't occasionally walk in off the street."

"Sure. And they demand to see Mr. Foley, Mr. Feinberg, or Mr. Chong. Either that, or they want directions to the washroom."

"Foley looks like a successful guy," John went on, undaunted. "Ever watched to see how he does it?"

"Whatever Foley does," Suzy replied, dripping sarcasm, "he does on the golf course during the day and at night clubs later on. What do you think? Should I join the country club or the disco circuit?"

John patted Suzy affectionately and retreated to his armchair. He had done battle with Suzy's slump and acknowledged defeat. Besides, it was time to watch "Laverne and Shirley."

Suzy continued to brood. It's one of "Murphy's Laws" (or if it isn't, it certainly should be) that when things look totally black there's an excellent chance they'll get even worse. Hubert had taught the salespeople to profit from their failures and catastrophes, to think of them as "educational experiences." In that spirit, be it noted that Suzy probably set the record for consecutive educational experiences in a 30-day period.

There was, for example, Mr. Simmons, a successful insurance executive. One of Suzy's friends tipped her off that he was thinking of selling his house and buying a condominium. Suzy arranged an appointment, researched the property, did her comparables, took pictures, and made a pluperfect listing presentation. Perfect except that she didn't get the contract signed. The next day, Buster called her into his office.

"This'll be hard to take, Suzy," he began. "I know you worked on the Simmons house. He called—said you were a charming young lady, but he prefers to work with someone . . . ah . . . more experienced. I've asked Harry to handle it."

"But that's not fair," Suzy cried. "Didn't you argue with him?"

"No point in it," Buster replied flatly. "Simmons is old school—can't adjust to talking business with a pretty woman. "Harry feels rotten about it. I'm sure he'll cut you in."

Suzy was close to tears. "That's not the point. Do I have to be old and ugly to have credibility—or is that a privilege reserved for men?"

"Only an old fossil like Simmons would feel that way," Buster assured her.

Suzy's next prospect was a very *young* man who wandered into the office during her opportunity time. However, he didn't appear to have a nickel in his jeans, and there was evidence that he didn't own a bar of soap either. Counting pencil stubs looked like a more productive endeavor than working with this unsavory specimen.

"May I help you?" Suzy asked. "Afraid we don't handle rentals in this office."

"I wanna buy," he replied, sprawling into a chair. "Something with lotsa class."

"Lotsa class means lotsa bucks, you know," Suzy said rather condescendingly.

"I can dig it! Nothing but the best for Johnny."

"Well, Johnny, I'm tied up today," Suzy said impatiently. "Maybe if you could come back tomorrow, someone can show you around."

A few days later word leaked back that Johnny had gone across the street to XYZ Realty—and bought an expensive house for cold cash. This elicited a tiresome tirade from Buster about judging people by appearances.

"Probably made his money growing marijuana," Suzy grumbled.

"I don't see what that has to do with it," Buster replied icily.

Then there was the day Helga asked Suzy to sit an open house for one of her listings. At last—something with real profit potential. Or so Suzy thought until she learned that the house, which Helga had described as "not in the greatest location," was miles from the center of town, comfortably nestled between the state penitentiary and the county garbage incinerator. Thanks a lot, Helga.

"At least it'll be easy to find," Harry chuckled. "Just follow the garbage trucks."

Finding it was easy, but pounding a sign into the hard-packed ground was a real challenge. Suzy hammered the sign, first with a shoe, then with a paperweight, and finally with a package of frozen pork chops. When it was at last upright, she smiled stoically despite a painfully bruised elbow and proceeded to the front door, where the key flatly refused to turn in the lock. Simultaneously, as if well rehearsed, the sign crashed down behind her and the doorknob came off in her right hand.

Just at that critical moment, another salesman pulled up with buyer prospects.

"Looks like you need some help, little lady," he smirked. "Now you just give me your hammer, and I'll take care of that sign for you."

"I don't have a hammer," Suzy replied. She hadn't felt quite so small since that day in the eighth grade when she'd gone to school with her dress on inside out.

"Of course, you don't. Ha ha. Probably wouldn't know which end of it to grab if you did, eh?" He delved into his trunk and pulled out a tool kit adequate for erecting a skyscraper.

"My 6-year-old son can do this," he added as he placed the sign with three mightly whacks of a sledge hammer.

Mr. Perfect replaced the doorknob and opened the door, which hadn't been locked in the first place. His people didn't care for the house at all, and Suzy spent the rest of the day nursing her elbow—undisturbed.

Still another educational experience was provided by Barbie, the perennial real estate exam taker. Thanks to luck or cheating, Barbie had finally made it on the seventh try. She was now an agent of the Golden Opportunity Land Sales Company.

"It's absolutely marvy," Barbie burbled. "Our dialers invite people to these groovy little cocktail parties. We show slides of Paradise Lake. Then, when they start to drool, we just sit around tables talking to them. We work in teams. I'm what we call an enthuser, and my partner's a closer. We split the commissions, of course. We've already sold 40 lots. Easy as pie."

Suzy felt very uncomfortable. Two years before, she'd attended a groovy little cocktail party and signed a contract to buy a lot in Palmtree Cove, Florida. Thorough old John had called a broker friend in Florida and discovered that Palmtree Cove was a salt marsh. It was undevelopable, often under water at high tide, and situated just 2 miles from the target area of a missile testing site. Fortunately, John had been able to rescind the contract. Otherwise, he might have rescinded the marriage license.

"Uh, Barbie, where is Paradise Lake? Have you seen it?" Suzy asked tentatively.

"Gosh, I'm not much for details, Suzy," Barbie replied. "I know it's near Wyoming. The pictures are really something. You and John oughta come have a look-see."

Suzy was certain that Paradise Lake would prove to be a two-frog puddle in a rattlesnake-infested desert. But Barbie obviously didn't know and couldn't care less. Suzy politely declined the invitation.

"How come," she asked John later, "that dizzy dame can sell one pothole after another, when I try so hard to be professional and come up empty-handed?"

John didn't have a ready answer. He made suitably sympathetic sounds, however, and offered a silent prayer that Suzy's slump would pass. It didn't.

Suzy reached her nadir the day she came home to find mother busily cleaning her house. Since mother never cleaned her own house, being possessed of an enviable cleaning woman, this unusual behavior was definitely intended to carry a not-so-subtle message. Matters progressed from bad to worse when they sat down for tea and small talk.

"Since you're so wrapped up in real estate," said mother, "you'll be interested to know that Aunt Margaret has decided to sell her house."

"Mother, that's terrific!" Suzy shouted. "I'll get in touch with her right away."

"Oh, don't trouble yourself, dear. She's already listed it with Redoubtable Realty."

Suzy was crushed. "Why in the world would she do that without even talking to me?" she wailed.

"I'm sure it didn't occur to her. After all, you can't expect us to take this whim of yours too seriously. You know, Suzy," mother continued in her go-to-your-room tone of voice, "you're a wife and a mother. Those responsibilities should come first. Besides, Margaret and I think it a poor practice to do business with relatives."

"It's a damned poor practice to even *have* relatives," Suzy muttered under her breath.

By now, Suzy had had enough of educational experiences. The time had come for resorting to last resorts. Her do-or-die plan was really very simple, a by-the-numbers approach. Suzy read one motivational book, listened to two how-to tapes, took three vitamin tablets, recited 10 Hail Marys, made 20 cold calls, then she set out to knock on each and every one of 300 doors in a 20-block area. She'd do it, she vowed, come rain, sleet, snow, locked gates, "no trespassing" signs, or even fierce watchdogs.

"This is a hammer."

The first day was tiring, the second exhausting. But on the third day, Suzy struck a mother lode. Randy was a tow-headed, freckle-faced 13-year-old. When she first saw him, he was sitting dejectedly on a curb, nursing a blistered heel. Poor kid. Suzy just had to stop and offer sympathy and first aid. They struck up a conversation, and it developed that Randy was the paper boy. He knew enough about the neighborhood and its occupants to satisfy the research requirements of the U.S. Census, the credit bureau, or an author bent on writing a new *Peyton Place*. For a $2-bill and a chocolate bar, Suzy acquired five leads. Within days she had two new listings and a buyer prospect in firm tow.

"Looks like our 'super' Suzy's back in high gear," Harry said at the next sales meeting. "What turned it around for you, honey— farming?"

"And a few other little tricks I've picked up!"

"Don't tell me you've bought a tool kit," he laughed.

"Sure, and even labeled the handles so I'll know which end to grab," she chuckled.

"Come on now—got a secret method you're not sharing with your old pals?" he teased.

"It's as old as the *Bible*, Harry," Suzy replied. "And a little child shall lead them."

"Am I supposed to make sense out of that?" he asked.

"Of course not. You aren't a mother," Suzy answered, giving him a friendly peck on the cheek.

No more slump. No more worrying about the piano payments. It was even possible to be polite (if not terribly cordial) to Aunt Margaret. Suzy was in love with the world and especially with tow-headed kids. She resolved to stay in close touch with Randy and keep him well supplied with chocolate bars. She also called the newspaper publisher to find out how old Mike would have to be before he could take on a delivery route.

READER'S QUIZ

This is a guaranteed foolproof quiz. All answers are correct. Give your-self a mark of 100, and brag a lot.

1. When a real estate saleswoman is obviously prosperous, the other agents in her company will assume that:

    _____ a. her rich uncle died.
    _____ b. her number came up in Las Vegas.
    _____ c. she's probably stealing their clients.
    _____ d. she ought to pick up the lunch checks.
    _____ e. other

2. When the saleswoman goes into a slump, the other agents

    _____ a. figure she ran out of luck (and never had talent).
    _____ b. try to steal her clients.
    _____ c. avoid having lunch with her.
    _____ d. rejoice.
    _____ e. other

3. When I'm in a slump, there's comfort to be found in
    _____ a. blaming my family.
    _____ b. kicking stray dogs.
    _____ c. seeing a gypsy fortune teller.
    _____ d. visiting a friendly bartender.
    _____ e. other

4. Typical of my educational experience is

    _____ a. the day my buyer prospect fell through the dining room floor of a termite-ridden house I was showing.
    _____ b. the day I found out my million-dollar investor was really a fugitive from a mental institution.
    _____ c. the day the title company found a $60,000-income-tax-lien on a $50,000-property I hoped to close.
    _____ d. the day I came home to find my competitor's "for sale" sign on my next-door-neighbor's house.
    _____ e. other

5. Saleswomen will usually acknowledge that men have superiority when it comes to

    _____ a. reaching high shelves.
    _____ b. carrying heavy boxes.
    _____ c. charming elderly ladies.
    _____ d. killing centipedes.
    _____ e. other

7
Clocks and Calendars Can't Wait

Her slump conquered and confidence restored, Suzy began to list and sell consistently. She found herself to be something of a perfectionist, driven by a conscience to devote meticulous care to every detail of the transaction and always studying to improve her competence. Clients appreciated her concern. Like all good salespeople, Suzy worked whenever they wanted her—nights, weekends, holidays, and often at the cost of skipped meals and lost sleep. The hours were long, but she loved it. As Will Rogers explained, "If you wouldn't rather be doing something else, it ain't work."

John didn't love it. He deplored tv dinners, growled when he couldn't find clean socks, played the martyr when he attended a PTA meeting alone, and waxed white-faced furious the night Suzy left her own dinner party to get a signature on a contract. He reached the end of his rope, however, the time she wheeled home at 2:00 A.M. after an extra-long session with a seller who was reluctant to accept a good offer.

"Dammit, Suzy, this was supposed to be a part-time job!" he shouted. "Don't you feel any obligation to this family anymore?"

Suzy was contrite. "Of course I do, and I'm sorry—but I have obligations to my clients, too. Please understand, John. How about if I come home early tomorrow, hum? We'll take the kids to the movies."

Peace was restored—temporarily. Suzy did get home early, and the gang was waiting for her. With the kids already in the car, John and Suzy were just closing the door when the phone rang.

"For God's sake, don't answer that," John warned.

"I have to, John. I've been trying to get hold of Mr. Edison for 3 days—it'll just take a second."

Mr. Edison was the tenant who occupied a house Suzy had listed. He didn't want it shown. The conversation went on and on as Suzy wheedled him down from abusive to just plain uncooperative and then finally to reluctantly acquiescent. Meanwhile John tapped his foot impatiently and groaned while Erin and Joey got into a screaming battle over who'd get to sit next to the window. Finally he removed the kids from the car and stalked into the kitchen to make them sandwiches. His promise of an outing another night provoked loud wails of violent protest.

When Suzy hung up she felt guilty, confused, and above all, exhausted. She thought back to the time she and Marjorie had sat over coffee comtemplating their newfound leisure. Was there ever really a time when a new day was a blank check—not an overdrawn account? Somewhere along the line, there must have been a happy medium, when the work at hand just comfortably filled the time available, and the things-to-do pile was polished off by sundown. If so, Suzy couldn't remember when that was. Now her desk harbored five intimidating piles of paperwork labeled:

- Urgent
- Must do today
- Must do this week
- As soon as possible
- Sooner or later

The last pile she called "the slag heap" because it grew bigger and uglier with each passing week. Ultimately, Suzy had come to share the businessperson's concept of an ideal office—one that would self-destruct every 3 months and thus afford her a new start.

"Don't say it, John," she said wearily when the children were finally tucked into bed. "I know this is getting out of hand. Please don't be angry—help me find a way to handle things better."

John was somewhat mollified. "You could accomplish just as much in half the time if you were better organized," he said. "You'll have to learn to plan. Establish priorities and eliminate wasted motion. Either that or kill yourself. I'll get you a book on time management."

"We studied that in training," Suzy recalled. "I'll look through my stuff and dig it out."

"Good," he said, warming up. "The first rule is to identify specific goals, and the second is to make a plan."

"Right—I remember that. Hubert even gave us action plan forms to fill out. Trouble is, we were too naive to know what to do with 'em— it was like plotting a trip to an unknown destination."

"Well, you know now. Do you still have the form?" he asked.

Suzy plowed through her desk and found a daily plan she'd filled out months ago. It was so beautiful it brought tears to her eyes:

6:00—7:00 A.M.   Exercise, bathe, dress, and eat a wholesome breakfast.

7:00—8:00 A.M.   Get the family off. Read the morning paper.

8:00—10:00 A.M.   Office time. Handle all phone calls, mail, paperwork, and research.

10:00—12:00   Go out and view new listings.

12:00—1:00 P.M.	Lunch with friend or inspirational book.
1:00—3:00 P.M.	Prospect for buyers, and show property.
3:00—4:00 P.M.	Make a listing presentation.
4:00—6:00 P.M.	Home. Prepare gourmet meal, rest, and change into something glamorous.
6:00—10:00 P.M.	Family time, or relax with friends. Early to bed.

"This is more like it," John said when he'd read it through. "It's sensible, organized—right to the point. Does away with all the mindless scurrying you do.

"I know, John," Suzy answered hesitantly. "The problem is . . ."

"No problem if you stick to this plan," John insisted. Don't stand still for unnecessary interruptions—that's the third rule.

"I'll try," Suzy promised, keeping her doubts to herself.

Unfortunately, the next morning began with an interruption. The tenant, Mr. Edison, called at 6:00 A.M. A pipe had burst, and his basement was rapidly flooding. He called back at 10-minute intervals to report on the rising tide, while Suzy contacted 17 plumbers on her other line. None was disposed to come immediately, and most had unkind, if not profane, things to say about early morning phone calls.

That crisis finally resolved, Suzy left for the office. The day had barely begun, and she was already formulating necessary revisions to her time management plan:

6:00—7:00 A.M.	Forget the exercises. Cope with the first three crises of the day in the order received. Drink coffee while on the phone. Try to squeeze in at least 10 minutes for showering and dressing, because leaving the house in bathrobe and rollers is considered definitely unprofessional.
7:00—8:00 A.M.	(or what's left of it) Wave good-bye to the family. Place the morning paper on the things-to-do pile; it probably doesn't have anything important in it, and if World War III has broken out, someone at the office is bound to mention it. On the other hand, you might tuck the paper under your arm. There'll be plenty of time to read it while stuck in rush-hour traffic.

John was right about one thing: avoiding unnecessary interruptions was the key. But how does one distinguish the unnecessary interruptions from the necessary ones? For example, mother's daily phone call and recitation of the litany of woes suffered by second, third, and even fourth cousins was probably nonessential. But it could hardly be prevented short of planting mother. An office is an interruption factory.

"Last night I had the strangest dream . . ."

Nonetheless, Suzy was still firmly resolved to get her schedule back on track. She had a long list of phone calls to be made first thing this morning. But she was greeted at the FFC door by Frances, a new agent with a friendly manner, pretty face, and nonstop mouth.

"You must be Suzy," Frances babbled. "Hubert told me to follow you around today and watch what you do. He says we have all kinds of things in common, like we're the same age and both married and have kids. Everybody thinks you're a total whiz. I'm so excited— well, actually, scared silly. I might have to run to the john to barf— but I'm really excited. Hubert thinks I have great potential."

"Marvelous. I'm flattered Hubert would think I could help," Suzy managed to say when she could squeeze in a word. She was torn between planning mayhem for Hubert and wondering whether a day in the Soldsine footsteps might bring an abrupt end to a budding career. Mainly, she was kind of hoping Frances would go barf so she'd at least have a chance to empty her message box.

Her train of thought was broken by a phone call from the plumber who'd fixed the broken pipe. Then, an irate call from Edison demanding to know who was going to pay the plumber's bill. Suzy thought this was a good question in view of the plumber's report that the broken pipe had been caused by Edison's kids playfully pounding nails into it. The conversation was colorful but not conclusive.

Another call, already on hold, proved to be more promising. A friend of John's indicated that his mother had decided to sell her house. Would Suzy come out immediately and discuss it? Suzy could vaguely remember having met Mrs. Caradine several years before. According to Caradine, Junior, she owned a large, colonial house in a charming residential neighborhood. So, with Frances merrily trotting alongside, Suzy grabbed her bag and whizzed out the door.

Enroute, she made a conscientious effort to explain to Frances that this is why listing presentations are not always amenable to scheduling between 3:00 and 4:00 in the afternoon. And why the competent agent can't always arrange to do the necessary research that should precede the presentation. For the most part, she settled for listening, and thus learned just about everything there was to know about Frances.

Mrs. Caradine met them at the door, wearing a flowered nightgown, not too surprising in view of the fact that the day was still relatively young. What was surprising, however, was the realization that Mrs. C. was obviously drunk as a lord. She held a cocktail glass in one hand and with the other made a sweeping gesture of welcome that almost caused her to topple over backwards.

"You musht be whatcha call it," she said cordially. "Jush help yourshelf to a drink an' show me where to shign."

"Yes, I'm Suzy Soldsine from FFC Realty," replied Suzy, trying desperately to retain her poise. "If you don't mind, we'd like to take a look around, and then perhaps we can get together with your son to discuss the listing."

"Look your head off," said Mrs. Caradine, heading back to the bar for a refill. "And leave that pompoush ash kid of mine out of it. Jush write the contract and show me where to shign."

"It's a question of establishing the correct price."

"Thash your problem," the dear lady barked. "You name the price and I'll shign."

For the better part of an hour, Mrs. Caradine pursued Suzy all around the house, loudly demanding that she be allowed to "shign" something. Suzy stoutly resisted even opening her briefcase. Only when they were back in the car did Suzy remember Frances, who was stunned into total silence.

"Relax, Frances," she laughed. "This wasn't exactly your typical listing situation."

Frances looked relieved, if not reassured.

Before returning to the office they called in for messages. A buyer for whom Suzy had written an offer was now having a virulent attack of the disease known as "Buyer's Remorse." They drove clear across town and spent an hour administering tender loving care.

"Gee, how'd you work that little miracle?" Frances asked afterwards. "They were set to cancel, and now you've got them purring like little kittens."

"They just needed a little starch poured in them. I reminded them of the reasons they decided to buy in the first place."

With the offer reinstated, there was barely enough time to get to a 1:00 P.M. closing.

Throughout the morning, Suzy continued pointing out to Frances (or was it rationalizing to herself?) why real estate work does not adapt to a rigid schedule. Meanwhile, Suzy's own daily plan was undergoing further revision:

8:00—10:00 A.M.   Get to the office and prepare to deal with several interruptions.

10:00—12:00   Deal with the interruptions to the interruptions.

12:00—1:00 P.M.   Best to skip lunch since this hour might occasionally afford you a chance to do some of the things you planned to do before you were interrupted.
Besides, skipping lunch is good for the figure.

After the closing, Buster had scheduled Suzy to pick up a buyer who was referred by an out-of-town broker. The customer proved to be a family of five, including two teenagers and a 10-year-old. They were being transferred to the city from a small, rural community in a neighboring state. Using two cars, Suzy and Frances drove them around various residential areas. Suzy quickly discerned that:

- they were totally unprepared for price levels in the city
- they were unable to buy at said higher levels
- they were disenchanted with everything they saw anyhow
- they were inclined to start every sentence with "Back in Rushville . . ."

After 3 hours and 77 back-in-Rushvilles, Suzy dropped them off at their motel.

"Will anything come of that?" Frances asked.

"I hope so, Suzy replied. "I hope he'll tell his boss to forget about the transfer, and move back to Rushville. Most of these out-of-town referrals turn out to be what I call *missionary runs.*"

"Yikes!" Frances shouted. "Look at the time, and I don't have a bloomin' thing in the house for supper."

"Don't worry," said Suzy soothingly. "There's a deli in the next block. I planned on stopping there anyhow."

"Is every day as busy as this one?" Frances asked plaintively.

"No indeed," Suzy replied. "Some are a helluva lot worse."

After supper, Suzy regaled John with anecdotes about Frances, the Rushville folks, and the morning habits of his friend's mother. They weren't interrupted. (Suzy had thoughtfully taken the phone off the hook.)

John, however, couldn't be sidetracked from the subject of time management. "Sounds like your plan got blown away," he grumbled.

"Suzy, if you allow yourself to be constantly derailed, you surrender control over your own life. Have you made a plan for tomorrow?"

Suzy considered having hysterics but settled for some mild sarcasm. "Sure I have. Tomorrow I'll do all the things I planned to do today. Matter of fact, that'll probably be the plan for day after tomorrow too, so I'm way ahead of you."

John wasn't amused. "You can put things off for just so long before they start catching up with you," he stated ponderously.

Suzy knew better than to reply. John was of the school that believes procrastination is a cardinal sin. For Suzy, both as a homemaker and as a salesperson, it had become a necessary way of life. In fact, if she ever wrote a book on time management she would undoubtedly entitle it *Creative Procrastination.*

To appease John, who was now wrapped up in the 11:00 news, Suzy dug out her time management notes again. Perhaps there was one useful nugget she'd missed. It all but leaped out at her: Rule 7—*Use services that will free time for you.*

Suzy knew better than to assume that FFC would supply such services. Not even Helga rated a favor from a stenographer. But Frances, heretofore a pesky chatterbox, now loomed large as a potential key chaser, comparables researcher, document carrier, and so forth.

On the other hand, the notion that Frances could be conned into stopping by to wash Suzy's breakfast dishes was too much to hope for. A housekeeper, though . . . Suzy's smile broadened as the idea grew in size and beauty. Sure, it would be expensive, but also enchanting. And, of course, it was decidedly motivational. She resolved to place an ad for a housekeeper the next day.

Thus encouraged, Suzy picked up her pencil and put the finishing touches on her own daily action plan:

1:00—5:00 P.M.   Roll with the punches. Be sure to reserve at least 15 minutes for stopping by a fast-food outlet on the way home. Also, 10 minutes for fresh lipstick and a dab of perfume. (If those perfumes are worth half the price and are a tenth as effective as the ads would have us believe, they should be capable of counteracting a husband's predictable response to another round of pastrami and potato salad.)

5:00—whenever   Judiciously divide attention between the family and clients you couldn't reach during the day. (After all, isn't this why God gave us two ears?) If husband complains about too many nights out with clients, remind him that *he* hasn't asked you out for dinner in weeks.

"Learning anything from all that busywork?" John asked affectionately as he got up to head for bed.

Suzy tucked her plan away. "I think I am—in fact, I may have just come up with a new definition of success. It's a matter of time."

"Mmm hmm—that's the secret of success all right," said John, stifling a yawn. "Just a matter of learning to program your time. You *are* a success, Suzy, and I'm proud of you."

Suzy beamed. She did indeed feel successful. From her point of view, though, success in real estate was defined as the height you've achieved when you stop worrying about how to manage your time and humbly admit that time is managing you.

READER'S QUIZ

This is a guaranteed foolproof quiz. All answers are correct. Give yourself a mark of 100, and brag a lot.

1. My time management philosophy is

_____ a. "Never put off till tomorrow, things you can do the day after tomorrow."

_____ b. "Never put off till day after tomorrow, things you can do next month."

_____ c. "Never put off till next month, things you can do after retirement."

_____ d. "Always put off indefinitely, things that, if put off, may never have to be done at all."

_____ e. other

2. I knew I had a time management problem when

_____ a. my dentist called to say I was 3 years late for my appointment.

_____ b. I didn't quite make it into bed before the alarm rang.

_____ c. my wardrobe became so out-of-date that it came back in style.

_____ d. I had to rent warehouse space for my in-basket.

_____ e. other

3. I could manage my time much better if

_____ a. I had three secretaries and an executive assistant.

_____ b. the accident prone could be kept off the freeway.

_____ c. the day could be lengthened to 72 hours.

_____ d. a plague would strike all my clients who are incapable of communicating during business hours.

_____ e. other

4. The telephone is a time saver, but the telephone company has not addressed the problem of people who

_____ a. never return your calls.

_____ b. have inadequate lines and endless busy signals.

_____ c. leave mysterious and undecipherable messages on your answering machine.

_____ d. put you on "hold" and play inane music in your ear.

_____ e. other

5. My best-loved time saver is

     ____ a.   a souped-up car.
     ____ b.   instant oatmeal.
     ____ c.   iron-on patches.
     ____ d.   my wastebasket.
     ____ e.   other

8
Beware the Ides of April

A fundamental axiom of real estate management holds that salespeople have a deep craving and dire need for recognition. Suzy sometimes wondered if the powers that be at FFC were aware of this. Weeks went by when everyone from top dog to lowliest underling was too busily ensconced in a personal orbit to give a damn whether she came or went. After watching the constant parade of salespeople leaving and new ones coming aboard, she doubted if half the staff even knew who she was. When management did single her out, it was usually to give her a tongue lashing for some educational experience she had endured.

Suzy's career did provide plenty of satisfaction. By the end of her first year in the business, she was among the company's top five producers. She took her listings at salable prices, and most of them sold. She learned to analyze her buyers' motivations with something close to ESP, and most of them bought. Clients liked Suzy's work and sent their friends to her. Other agents sought her out when they needed advice or a kind word. Not the least of her satisfaction was the steady stream of commission checks.

"I've opened my own bank account," Suzy told Frances proudly. "John said I should."

"That's terrific," Frances replied. "But I hate banks. They look like mausoleums."

"That's the whole idea," Suzy laughed. "Makes us poor peasants feel even poorer in the presence of those almighty dollars."

"Yeah—especially when we've come in to argue about the statement or explain why we're overdrawn," Frances added. She raised her coffee cup in the air. "Here's to the day I put more in than I take out! Does it give you the right to spit in their eye?"

"Mmm, no. Come to think of it, I still tremble at the teller's window."

"Then, to hell with working! Let's go out and buy some clothes," Frances suggested. "Something outrageous to wow 'em at the banquet."

The banquet was the talk of the office. Apparently, Foley,

Feinberg, and Chong had indeed read their textbooks on management and saw it as their responsibility to give out heaping measures of praise and recognition. Said reinforcement was all bound up in one gala affair, the annual awards banquet—a lavish dinner-dance at the country club with fresh flowers for the ladies, entertainment, and a staggering array of prizes for which the more competitive agents were evidently prepared to steal, maim, or kill. Real estate agents, even those who are mathematically retarded, have an uncanny ability to calculate commissions with breathless speed and unerring accuracy. The names of those in contention were no secret.

Suzy's latent competitive instincts had been thoroughly trampled on during her high school days. She'd never once made honor roll, been elected to class office, or earned an athletic award. Philosophically, she'd learned that life without fame can nevertheless be satisfying as long as one passes every grade, stays out of jail, and is assured of a date for Saturday night. When it was rumored that this year's prize for "top producer" would be a trip for two to Acapulco, Suzy did feel a tiny competitive stir. But the notion that anyone could beat Helga to this plum wasn't even worth considering.

"You'll beat her, Suzy—maybe not this year but soon," Harry assured her. "And she knows it. Watch out for arsenic in your coffee cup."

For now, Suzy had to put that goal on the back burner. The banquet would be a fun party and a great opportunity to introduce John to her new "family." John was less than equally enthusiastic, especially when he learned he'd have to rent a tuxedo.

"My contempt for stiff shirts is exceeded only by my feelings about banquet food," he snarled.

"So wear a soft shirt, and eat a ham sandwich before you go."

He wasn't appeased. "I won't know a soul. And look at the stupid way they've addressed this invitation: 'Suzy Soldsine and spouse.' Some fool will probably plaster me with a name tag that reads 'Mr. Suzy.'"

Suzy refrained from mentioning how many times she'd gone by the name of Mrs. John. Being a spouse is evidently a role reserved for wives. She felt confident, though, that feminine persuasion would get John to the club and that a few stiff drinks would see him and his tux through the evening.

It was a spectacular night for the FFC crew. The party began with a cocktail hour, followed by three courses of food that lived up to John's expectations in every respect: tardy service, tepid temperature, and tough meat. In spite of that—or because of the open bar—a festive mood prevailed.

Hubert, wearing a brocade dinner jacket in shades of purple and puce, acted as master of ceremonies.

"Good evening, salespeople—and all you order takers, too," he began.

The audience chuckled politely.

"Anyone know where I can get an 8 percent loan for an unemployed welder with six kids?" he went on.

"Is this supposed to be funny?" John whispered to Suzy.

Hubert introduced Mr. Chong, who managed to say a few words without once mentioning paper clips. Then Mr. Foley made a lengthy and sentimental speech declaring his deep affection and undying gratitude for each and every agent, who were like sons and daughters to him.

"Yeah, whether he knows our names or not," Frances giggled. "I have yet to meet the guy."

Mr. Feinberg settled for telling them that he was working on "something really big" and that they would be hearing all about it in the "very near future." Finally, with much fanfare, Hubert began announcing awards and distributing prizes. First came plaques and bonus checks for the 17 agents who made the "million dollar club." This list included both Suzy and Clara. John was duly impressed.

"Always wanted to be married to a millionairess," he teased.

"Well, you'd better keep working on it," Suzy laughed. "This just means we've listed or sold more than a million dollars worth of property. No great shakes in this market."

Suzy wasn't particularly surprised when she was named "rookie of the year." But she was overwhelmed when thunderous applause greeted the announcement that she'd been voted "most cooperative" by the other agents.

After that, practically everything went to Helga, with Harry a perennial second. The big finale was something of a letdown. Only perfunctory clapping greeted Helga's crowning as "top producer." She accepted her prize with curt condescension—as if she'd already tired of Acapulco and would have preferred Paris or Rome.

"If this were the Oscars, she would at least thank a few dozen people for making it possible," John muttered.

Suzy laughed. "I can't imagine Helga feeling that anyone else helped. Except possibly the telephone company."

"She probably owns that, too," Frances added.

John was rather quiet on the way home. "You were wonderful, John," Suzy ventured. "Meeting all those high-powered salespeople must have been overwhelming."

"They're nice people," John replied. "I can see why you enjoy working with them. What I can't get used to is the way you all throw dollar signs around."

"Guess that does come off as rather tacky. But that's the language of our business. Your tractors and bulldozers have set prices; with real estate, we're constantly negotiating."

"I understand that. But the level of earnings blows my mind. Harry said Helga made about $90,000 this past year."

"Sure, but there aren't many like Helga. If it'll make you feel better, I can name quite a few who didn't earn the price of a can of peanuts."

"But it's possible to make that much—and you might very well be one of the ones who can," John said. "Better plan on staying home tomorrow," he added as they drove into their driveway. "We've got to have a look at our income taxes. It's that time of year again."

Suzy cringed. Past years' experience had taught her that looking at taxes was a tortuous exercise calculated to turn a normally kind and courteous man into a raging beast. She'd never been able to understand why John worried so much about taxes, when they always wound up getting money back. In fact, she'd come to think of income taxes as a generous windfall from a benevolent government. Suzy had never actually made out the return. In fact, the sum total of her tax knowledge was derived from watching H & R Block commercials on tv.

The next morning she delved into her checkbooks and itemized her deductible expenses.

"You'll be pleased, John," she said brightly. "It's a much longer list now that I'm working."

"I hope so," he replied. "You've undoubtedly pushed us into a higher bracket. Get me your W-2 form."

"Are men ever satisfied?" Suzy wondered silently. She also wondered what and where a W-2 form might be. John read her puzzled expression.

"The W-2 form, Suzy, is a little slip of paper the company gives you. It shows how much you made last year and how much income tax was deducted."

"They don't deduct taxes from our commissions, John," Suzy exclaimed. "I know that for a fact. Once, a new payroll clerk deducted stuff from one of Helga's checks—almost lost an arm for it."

"Oh, Lord," John moaned. "Then you must have a 1099. I only hope to hell somebody around there taught you about filing estimated tax returns."

"Hubert gave us a little pamphlet about that," Suzy recalled. "It said you should base your estimate on last year's earnings. But I didn't make anything last year."

One look at John's face, and Suzy scurried to her desk. She found the 1099 on the slag heap in a bulging folder labeled "to be filed." It revealed that she had been paid $21,000. John greeted this news as if it were a major disaster. The situation obviously called for more patience than he was capable of mustering. They decided to call in an accountant.

The prospect of visiting an accountant's office was as intimidating to Suzy as a trip to the bank. She felt abysmally ignorant and faintly guilty. The next day at work she asked if anyone knew of a good book on income taxes.

"Why don't you just go to the Internal Revenue Service office," Frances suggested brightly. "They have people there who can answer all your questions. I heard that on the radio this morning."

Harry seemed to think this was hysterically funny. But Suzy did go to the IRS office. She was somewhat comforted by the long lines of poor souls who obviously found the annual tax exercise as mystifying as she did. Unfortunately, the waiting in line proved totally unproductive. Once she got to the front, she couldn't think of anything specific to ask.

Later, en route to the accountant's office, John was careful to remind Suzy that professional people charge by the hour—and through the nose. It wasn't really necessary because accountants are too busy in the month preceding April 15 to indulge in idle chitchat. They're also too busy to eat and sleep, which has a tendency to make them grumpy.

Suzy was impressed with the competent way the CPA leafed through the bundle of papers they'd brought. She hoped she had supplied logical answers to the multitude of sticky questions he asked:

ACCOUNTANT: Why don't you charge your gasoline on a credit card so you can keep track of expenditures?

SUZY: Because my car hasn't sense enough to run out of gas within coasting distance of a Texaco station.

ACCOUNTANT: Why don't you charge those lunches and dinners that you have with clients and other agents, and make a note of your guests?

SUZY: McDonald's doesn't take Master Charge.

ACCOUNTANT: Why don't you keep receipts for parking fees?

SUZY: Meters don't give receipts. You're lucky if they even take the money.

"Well, John," said the accountant at last, as if Suzy weren't even present, "if the little lady wants to continue being a big earner, I think she'll need a manager. And you're going to need some tax shelter."

Suzy just wished the man would stop making "tsk tsk" sounds. But he seemed capable of clearing up the immediate problem, and John was resigned to watching over Suzy's personal accounting for the time being. Everything was OK—except that the immediate problem was going to cost them something like $4,000 in taxes, penalties, and fees.

A quick survey of the latest bank statements revealed that John and Suzy were just about $3,000 short of the required amount. This provoked another unfortunate series of questions about where the blankety blank $21,000 had gone. Despite the piano, a new car, some necessary clothes, and the exorbitantly expensive babysitters and itinerant cleaning ladies, Suzy herself was mystified.

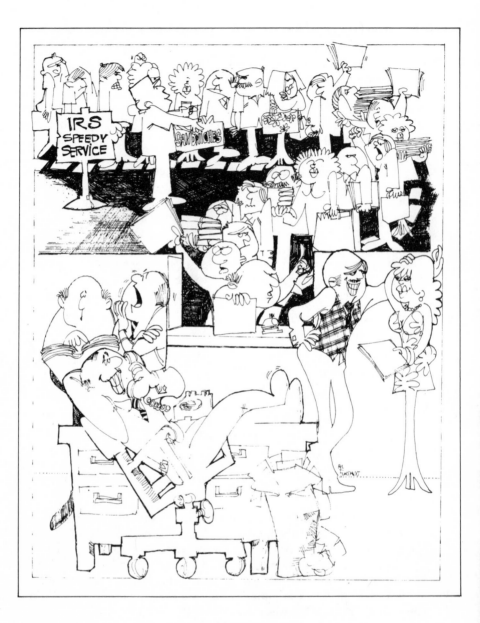

The friendly folks at the tax office.

"I know I made a large deposit about 3 weeks ago," she said. "The bank must have made a mistake."

"Sure they did," John said sarcastically. "Or maybe you haven't gotten around to telling me about your latest extravagance."

Suzy was hurt. "It's there, John. I'll stop at the bank tomorrow."

"Good. But if it isn't there, you'd better ask for a loan."

The domestic climate was still cool, and Suzy was understandably depressed when she left for work the next day. At the sales meeting, Mr. Feinberg finally revealed all the details about the something really big he and Joel had been massaging for many months: FFC was going to build and market a 30-story condominium building in the heart of downtown. There would be 300 apartments selling for an average price of $50,000 each.

"Just think, gang," Hubert shrieked in wild enthusiasm, "Crystal Cliff is $15 million worth of inventory, and it's all yours. Just wheel in 300 buyers, and we can all retire."

The staff had to undergo special training for the project. They were given huge packets of papers containing architectural drawings, advertising materials, and sheets of endless numbers showing projected maintenance fees, taxes, mortgage payments, and other expenses for every unit. They pondered the legal documents, a wondrous collection of words like "whereas" and "hereinafter," interspersed with cryptic phrases such as "except as noted in paragraph *m*."

"One comforting thought," Harry offered, "the clients won't understand this stuff either."

Least comprehensible of all was the little talk Joel gave on investor purchasers. He used the example of a person who would buy with a minimum down payment and thus incur monthly costs of about $600. The apartment wouldn't rent for more than $400 a month, but Joel insisted that the investor would nevertheless be tickled pink because of the depreciation and also because of the appreciation. Suzy couldn't quite believe that Mr. Feinberg and his computer had invented a miraculous apartment that could rise and fall in value simultaneously. She wondered if Joel had ever marketed one of those revolutionary diet plans— the ones that guarantee weight loss while allowing you to stuff yourself with eggs Benedict and Vienna pastry.

"Joel," she asked later when she cornered him alone, "can you run that by me once more—the part about how the guy can be so pleased at losing $2,400 per year?"

"It's called a tax shelter, baby, and it's the best kind going. That $2,400 he loses comes home to papa in the form of about $4,000 in savings on income taxes. Does that make sense?"

"Wow, does it ever!" Suzy shouted. "Joel, honey, you may not know it, but you've just made your first sale."

"A little check for a mere $10,000, and it's all yours."

That reminded Suzy that she had to stop at the bank. As usual, her confidence drained away with every further step inside the marble edifice. Suzy's pleas, threats, and tears failed to swerve the banker's conviction that neither he nor his computer had recorded a large deposit for the previous month.

"Guess I'll have to get a loan, then," Suzy sighed. "I need it to pay taxes."

"Yes, well, we'll have to see your tax returns to verify your income," the banker said sternly.

"Why in the world would I need money for taxes if I didn't have income?" Suzy exclaimed.

The banker looked heavenward in despair and handed her some loan application forms. Later, back at the office, Suzy was embarrassed but also elated to find a note from Mrs. Niggardly in her message box asking when she intended to pick up the check that had been lying around for weeks. Suzy resolved to open a new account in another bank, the one that advertised "friendly and neighborly service." Her feeling of grievance was thus adjudicated, and the tax payment was assured. John never did hear the whole story, as it didn't seem worth the effort of going into tiresome details.

"The money's there, John, just like I said," she told him that evening. "We have more than enough. Besides, I think I've turned up a good tax shelter."

John looked relieved—and also surprised. "Tax shelter? What do you know about tax shelters?"

"I know about real estate, John," Suzy said gently, "and what better tax shelter can you find? FFC's building a condo project. . . ."

Suzy pulled out the data sheets Joel had given her, and John went through them carefully with growing interest.

"Of course, it'll take $10,000 down," Suzy began somewhat doubtfully. "Maybe mother'd like to go halves."

"Good location," John was mumbling." And the numbers make sense. Forget about your mother; we can probably swing this. Do you get a commission for selling to yourself?"

"Of course. That's one of our fringe benefits."

"So that'd take care of part of the down. It's not a bad investment at that."

Suzy was jubilant. John talked it over with Mr. Feinberg himself on the following day and decided to buy. They were not, however, the first Crystal Cove purchasers, but the sixth. Helga had sold five units while Suzy was at the bank.

READER'S QUIZ

This is a guaranteed foolproof quiz. All answers are correct. Give your-self a mark of 100, and brag a lot.

1. A real estate company's annual awards dinner is an occasion when

    _____ a.   agents who haven't appeared all year finally emerge from hiding.
    _____ b.   the bosses pat all the agents on the back (and the office help on the fanny).
    _____ c.   plaque manufacturers declare a dividend.
    _____ d.   the disenchanted strive mightily to drink up the company's profits.
    _____ e.   other

2. No matter how skimpy the commission check, the prudent agent should always reserve enough cash to pay

    _____ a.   the parking meter.
    _____ b.   the pay toilet.
    _____ c.   the bar bill.
    _____ d.   gambling debts.
    _____ e.   other

3. I wish I could find a bank that would

    _____ a.   staff the nine teller windows with at least six tellers instead of two.
    _____ b.   make me a loan without first requiring that I prove I don't need it.
    _____ c.   just once issue a statement that agrees with the number in my checkbook.
    _____ d.   offer customers the same prompt response they give to holdup men.
    _____ e.   other

4. The kind of assistance I usually get at the tax office can best be described as

    _____ a.   commendable.
    _____ b.   debatable.
    _____ c.   regrettable.
    _____ d.   incredible.
    _____ e.   other

5.   Income tax problems have led me to

_____ a.   welcome natural disasters and unprofitable ventures.
_____ b.   become the parent of 16 children.
_____ c.   serve a term in a federal penitentiary.
_____ d.   quit working.
_____ e.   other

9
Not Tonight, Dear –
I Have an Appointment

Suzy had now reached what Hubert called "the level of conscious competence." She could work her way through the intricacies of a residential transaction with the aplomb of a frog hopping lily pads.

Shortly after she and John bought the first condo, they decided to take a second, using commissions Suzy had earned on 10 others. And there were additional kinds of success. With Frances launched on a promising career, Suzy took on a succession of other neophytes. It was time-consuming, but she enjoyed it almost as much as her saleswork. Suzy knew she'd arrived, because Mr. Foley hugged her often, and Helga was becoming increasingly hostile. Life was utterly delicious, except for Suzy's growing guilt pangs about neglecting her family.

To compound the problem, Eloise phoned, begging Suzy to help at the Board of Realtors®.

"I've been tapped for programs chair again, dammit! Suzy, I need your help."

"Oh, Eloise, I'm so confounded busy already. . . ."

"Who isn't?" Eloise interrupted. This committee is a rare bunch, believe me. They come late, leave early, and are constantly running to the phone in between. All we do is plan the monthly membership luncheons. Boils down to four simple questions: where to eat, what to eat, what to discuss, and who to get as speaker.

"Doesn't sound too challenging," Suzy replied tentatively.

"You wouldn't think so—well, here's the rub: if we choose a posh place and have a lavish meal, about 30 percent will be delighted and 70 percent will complain about the price. On the other hand, if we go to Dino's Diner, 30 percent will be pleased and 70 percent will complain about indigestion."

"Let me get this straight," Suzy said. "Are you saying 40 percent are never satisfied?"

"Right on, cookie. And that doesn't even take into account the 80 percent of our membership who never show. Don't bother about the never-satisfieds, though. Complaining's what they do best."

"Seems to me a good speaker is more important than the food," Suzy ventured.

"Ah, that's the other rub," Eloise replied. "Put on an entertainer, and the intellectuals mumble about more meat. Put on meat, and the lightweights nod off."

"Can't a speaker be a little of both?" Suzy asked.

"You're talking about a rare bird—and an expensive one. My budget is a big zilch, so I'm stuck with middle-echelon bankers and bureaucrats who are neither very wise nor witty. What's worse, the freebies have a nasty way of canceling out at the eleventh hour if something more lucrative comes along."

"I don't envy you, Eloise," Suzy said sympathetically. "Why do you let yourself in for such a thankless job?"

"It's temporary, hon," Eloise replied. "When Henry Kissinger gets his real estate license, the post is all his."

"Well, count me in, then. For better or for worse," Suzy laughed.

It turned out to be for worse. It was a committee meeting that detained Suzy the evening she and John were supposed to have dinner with John's boss.

"John, you won't believe the ridiculous argument we got into," she began as she burst into the house, breathless and apologetic.

"He's gone, mom," Mike told her. "Said you shouldn't worry about it—he'll tell them you have the flu."

Suzy spent a miserable evening. John came home very late and shrugged off her apologies as if it didn't matter. The next day, Suzy persuaded Clara to pinch-hit at an open house so that she could stay home. But John was preoccupied and spent most of the day in the bedroom with his nose in a book.

Suzy made a conscientious effort to come home early all during the week that followed. John was late on Monday, and on Tuesday he called to say he wouldn't make it home for dinner at all.

"John, it's been ages since we've been out for dinner, just the two of us," she suggested. "How about Thursday?"

"Sure, fine," he replied absentmindedly.

But Thursday brought a major hassle at the office. An irate buyer threatened to sue FFC, Suzy, and everyone else within range because he'd been told his sewer was connected and found that it wasn't.

"It's not my fault, Buster," Suzy wailed. "The seller said it was connected and so did the sewer department. What was I supposed to do, dig up the damned yard?"

"Just keep cool. They're on their way with a battery of legal talent. Let Chong do the talking."

"Reluctantly, Suzy called home to tell John she'd be delayed.

"He isn't here, mom," Mike told her. "He called to say he'd be working late again tonight."

Suzy called John's office, but he wasn't there. The man who answered

chuckled when she asked if he knew where John might be. He didn't.
She called again later. No answer.

The meeting with the sewerless buyers was long and difficult, but
Mr. Chong handled it well. Suzy got home before John did. When he
arrived, it was obvious he'd forgotten about the dinner date. He tossed
out a vague apology and an unconvincing explanation about where he'd
been.

Trouble—with a capital *T*. In 14 years of double harness, Suzy'd
never experienced it. Sure, they'd had their share of troubles with a
small *t:* routine go-rounds about leaving the car headlights on all
night, taking dirty socks off in the living room and expecting someone
else to pick them up, serving cauliflower three times in one week, or
dancing all night with a dizzy redhead. That kind of trouble comes on
like a thunderstorm and disappears just as quickly. It cleans the air,
relieves the monotony, and also clears the sinuses.

Trouble with a big *T* just kind of sneaks up. No one can ever
remember exactly when it began.

"It's serious," Suzy confided to Eloise. "John isn't being John.
I had my hair cut short, and he didn't even notice. What'll I do?"

"Do? Forget it. Ignore it. Men have their moods, too, y'know.
How about coming with us to San Francisco?"

"Are you out of your mind?"

"Probably, but not about this. A bunch of us are going to the
National Association of Realtors® convention. Clara said she'd come,
and Frances, too. We'll have a marvelous time, and you'll forget this
hoopla—or if you don't you can always jump off the Golden Gate
Bridge."

"Conventions—ugh! I went with John once to the road builders'
meeting," Suzy recalled. "Bunch of drunken men acting like oversexed
sophomores. Even a retired schoolteacher on a wooden leg would have
gotten the scare of her life."

"Or the thrill, as the case may be," Eloise added. "This is different.
Nice people. Terrific speakers. You'll learn a lot."

"Maybe next year," Suzy offered.

"Besides that, dammit, we'll have some fun," Eloise continued undaunted. "When was the last time you got away without the family
and kicked up your heels? Fun isn't necessarily synonymous with *sin*,
Suzy."

"Of course not," Suzy agreed quickly. "So why do I already feel
guilty?" she asked herself.

The idea was entrancing, and Eloise was persuasive. Suzy decided to
broach it to John and play it by ear, having first assembled arguments
for coping with opposition of the first, second, or third degree. As it
turned out, John was busily writing in a notebook. He greeted her news
with an mmm-hmmm response that would have been more appropriate
if she'd announced she was going upstairs to change her shoes.

"Eloise feels it'll help my career, John," Suzy continued in an attempt to pry John out of his work. "It's very educational."

"I'll bet."

On an impulse, she asked, "Would you like to go along?"

"Hell, no!" John replied vehemently.

"It isn't really all that important. If you'd rather I stayed home . . ."

"Don't be silly. Go, for cripe's sake. Have fun," John growled.

This uncharacteristic behavior could possibly be attributed to three helpings of lasagna. On the other hand, it had all the earmarks of an inkling. Suzy tried to peek over John's shoulder, to see what he was writing. He quickly shut his book and went upstairs.

At the office, Harry supplied the convenient shoulder to cry on.

"It's a strange and changing world, Suzy," he said thoughtfully. "I can remember when the typical plot was boy meets girl, boy loses girl, boy gets girl—and they lived happily ever after. Now it reads: boy marries girl, girl goes after career, girl leaves the slob because he's an obstacle in her path."

"So—and then what?"

"Then she revels in her independence or else looks for a guy who'll contract to do the dishes on Tuesdays, Thursdays, Saturdays, and alternate Sundays. Don't you read *Cosmopolitan?*"

"Not very often. I can't relate to that stuff about how important it is to wax your legs before flying off to the Bahamas for a weekend with your boss," Suzy replied, somewhere between laughter and tears.

Harry chuckled too. Then, again in his serious tone, he said, "Don't think it's easy mixing a career and marriage. It's like trying to crack walnuts while you're swinging from a trapeze."

"You seem to do all right."

"I know it sounds trite, but men are different. My wife balances the inconvenience of my crazy hours against her passion for spending my money. She's never threatened my delicate ego by going out and making a bundle herself. I'm not sure I'd take kindly to that."

"John encouraged me to work," Suzy argued. "He's very supportive—up to a point."

"Aha!" Harry shouted. "That's just it. Helga, for example, is forever passing the point. She has three divorces to prove it."

"Don't compare me with Helga, please," Suzy cried.

"Sorry—that wasn't fair. But look around you, Suzy. How many stable marriages do you see? I'm thinking the vows should be amended to read: 'for better or for worse, or until you catch athlete's foot, trump my ace, run out of toilet paper, or forget to pick up my Dior panty hose on the way home.'"

"Oh Harry, why don't I just have it out with John—ask him what the hell's going on?" Suzy asked.

"Maybe you're afraid to find out," Harry suggested.

"Maybe you're right."

In spite of Harry, in spite of John, and in spite of trouble, Suzy went to San Francisco with Eloise, Clara, and Frances. They had a ball. With the indefatigable Eloise in command, they sat through dozens of speeches and workshops, exchanged cards with thousands of Realtors, and staggered back to the hotel with shopping bags full of notes and handouts.

"You were right, Eloise," Suzy admitted, rubbing her feet. "I've learned a lot. These Realtors work hard."

"Yes, and play, too. Let's get changed and go sniff out the hospitality suites," Eloise suggested.

"How do you know where to find them?" Frances asked.

"No problem. You can hear them three floors away."

They wined, dined, and danced, then gabbed till dawn. Suzy hadn't had so much fun or so little sleep since her days at Sigma Chi house parties.

In what they came to call "the dorm," Suzy got to know her fellow saleswomen much more intimately. Inevitably, the husbands were a major topic of conversation. Suzy confessed her fears.

"Suzy, you can't believe that!" Frances was visibly upset. John—he adores you."

"It isn't John's fault. Maybe I've got my priorities scrambled."

"No way, baby," Eloise interrupted. "Suzy, you're bending this all out of proportion. Wait till you get back from this trip. You know what they say—absence makes the heart . . . "

"Barry's the most important thing in my life," Frances said. "If I thought I was losing him because of my job, I'd quit cold. I might even die."

"Well, quit first, please. We've already got too many dead sales-people," quipped Eloise.

"Eloise," Suzy said thoughtfully, "you seem to have this marriage and career thing all worked out. What's your secret?"

"It's the old infernal triangle, my dear: man, woman, and sewer connection," Eloise replied with a twinkle.

"This isn't funny!" Frances cried. "Suzy needs our help."

Clara had been rather quiet up to now. "Yes, tell us, Eloise. How do you and George manage it?"

"Fair exchange," Eloise said matter-of-factly. "I'm a reliable wage earner, and George is perennially unemployed. He needs my income, and I need his various services. Got it?"

"Gosh, that sounds so cynical," said Frances in dismay.

"No, just practical," Eloise replied. "I didn't mean to pop your balloon, but I threw away my Prince Charming illusions shortly after losing my virginity. My setup suits me fine."

Clara pulled the real shocker when she revealed she had been married for 24 years and was now separated. Somehow, they had always assumed she was single.

A convention is an "educational experience."

"Good Lord, Clara! What happened?" they chorused.

"A familiar story. My dignified lawyer turned into Menopause Marvin—an aging adolescent chasing young girls in bikinis—everything but the acne. I told him to shape up or ship out. He shipped."

"That's usually a temporary thing. He'll get over it," said Suzy sympathetically.

"He did. I didn't," said Clara with finality.

"Here's to men," Eloise yawned, heading for bed. "Love 'em or leave 'em, but always survive 'em."

Suzy flew home from San Francisco a renewed woman, thanks to having spent most of her last day in a spa. Trouble came crowding back, though, before she even got past the baggage area. John was supposed to meet the plane. He never showed. Since no one answered when she called the house, Suzy had to settle for a cab.

John came home much later and mumbled a weak excuse. He seemed exhausted. All the little stories Suzy'd been saving to tell him fell with dull thuds.

"Things being as they are," Suzy told Eloise a week or so later, "I wonder if he'll even remember that tomorrow's my birthday."

"He will if you use my foolproof method," Eloise replied. "I post signs all over the house and prime the kids to give George suggestions about appropriate gifts. Maybe you're *hoping* John won't remember."

"What kind of crack is that?"

"The old martyr game, baby—probably started with Eve. You're disturbed. Mr. Perfect isn't acting like Mr. Perfect these days. So, if he flubs the birthday, your cup runneth over with righteous indignations. It gives you a legitimate excuse for the explosion you so obviously need."

"That's too devious for me, Eloise."

"Not at all—simple as grits."

Despite her concern, Suzy's birthday wasn't overlooked. At breakfast John and the kids regaled her with a loud rendition of the traditional song. Mike presented her with a scout knife; Erin lovingly tendered an ashtray with her school picture glued to the bottom; and Joey proudly came forth with a lump of clay into which he'd embedded a dead beetle. Mother called to say she'd bring a cake for supper.

"I know you won't find time to bake one," she remarked.

"Why should I bake my own cake?" Suzy asked.

"Indeed, I don't know, since you don't even do it for the children anymore."

Suzy hung up, exasperated. After the kids had caught their bus, John poured another cup of coffee and sat down again. He handed Suzy an envelope. A greedy little voice inside was already saying, "A card? No gift?" She suppressed it. And an angry voice whispered, "If he's enclosed a check because he was too busy to shop—scream!" Her hand was trembling.

The card was your run-of-the-mill Hallmark—pastel flowers and a poem to match. Suzy almost overlooked the slip of paper that tumbled out. Its printed message was also short and sweet. John Andrew Soldsine had *passed* the real estate license examination.

Suzy was flabbergasted. "John, you turkey!" she shouted when she finally found her voice. "Is this why you've been staying out nights?"

"Going to school, honey. I wanted to surprise you. Wouldn't you know your plane came in the day of the state exam?"

"Do you realize I thought you were having an affair—with someone who looks like Farrah Fawcett Whatsername? I was ready to kill!"

John laughed, "Farrah has skinny legs and messy hair. Not my type at all. I happen to prefer Suzy. Didn't you know?"

With that, Suzy started to cry, "Oh, John, I've been an idiot!"

"You certainly have," John smiled.

"It's just that my life's changed so drastically. I sometimes wonder if I know myself anymore. Please forgive my jealousy trip."

"There's nothing to forgive. Guess I've been jealous, too—of your success. I want to be part of it, at least on the fringe."

"Oh, John," Suzy said, again, beaming through her tears.

"What's the chance of one idiot taking another out to lunch today?"

"Terrific! I'm due for a long, sinful, calorie-laden debauch."

"Pick you up at noon?"

"Not even a sewer connection could keep me away!"

READER'S QUIZ

This is a guaranteed foolproof quiz. All answers are correct. Give yourself a mark of 100, and brag a lot.

1.   A career woman should choose a husband who is

_____ a.   a career man.
_____ b.   a good cook.
_____ c.   a saint.
_____ d.   out-of-town.
_____ e.   other

2.   I knew my marriage was in trouble when

_____ a.   he announced a business trip to Seattle and bought two tickets to Las Vegas.
_____ b.   I found bikini pants in his raincoat pocket.
_____ c.   he came home late for dinner—4 days late.
_____ d.   he talked in his sleep about Sophia, and my name is Joan.
_____ e.   other

3.   When a marriage is in trouble, women friends will usually

_____ a.   tell a sadder story.
_____ b.   steer me to a suitable soap opera.
_____ c.   recommend a good attorney.
_____ d.   move in.
_____ e.   other

4.   In today's world, it sometimes seems that marriage is

_____ a.   precarious.
_____ b.   tempestuous.
_____ c.   superfluous.
_____ d.   ridiculous.
_____ e.   other

5.   I could successfully balance marriage and a career if I could only

_____ a.   keep the cleaning lady happy.
_____ b.   send my income to a numbered Swiss account.
_____ c.   maintain a generous supply of pep pills.
_____ d.   walk on water.
_____ e.   other

10

I'm Too Busy – Ask Your Father

John planned to limit his real estate activities to helping Suzy out on occasional weekends. FFC had a firm policy against accepting part-time agents, but they were willing to bend it in his case. They even allowed him to skip the training sessions on the grounds that he'd probably absorbed most of it by osmosis. Suzy was thrilled to have him aboard, as were the rest of the staff, with the exception of Helga. Helga raised a big issue about whether John's earnings would be attributed to Suzy for competition purposes. Buster assured her that they wouldn't. Even so, Suzy's listings were now "our listings," Suzy's buyers "our buyers." But this aura of family solidarity apparently didn't extend to the children.

"With both of you in this crazy business, we might as well be declared orphans," Mike complained. Mike was now going on 14. Taller than Suzy, he was beginning to sprout a shadow on his upper lip and was acquiring a voice that gravitated between boy soprano and amorous bull.

John was conciliatory, "My whole purpose in this, Mike, is to give your mother more time at home. We'll be able to alternate weekend appointments."

"And since when do you cherish having parents around?" Suzy added. "Seems to me you're never home except to raid the fridge."

"Yes, and where were you Saturday when I needed help with the lawn?" John asked.

"You'll have to stand in line, dad," Mike replied. "Most of my time's taken up babysitting the brats. And if that isn't the pits! There ought to be a law against making boys babysit."

"Boys grow up to be fathers," John suggested.

"Not if I can help it."

"Never mind," Suzy intervened. "We'll be getting another house-keeper next week. I have some interviews lined up."

The subject of housekeepers wasn't exactly fortuituous. Having made the decision sometime back to get full-time household help, Suzy had, in desperation, hired the first applicant who answered her ad.

Martha was painfully shy, chewed bubble gum, and wore carpet slippers. (Mother was appalled and said so, often.) Nonetheless, it was a lucky star that sent them Martha. She kept the house in order, cooked like Julia Child, and mended her way through a 3-year backlog without even being asked. Suzy had barely adjusted to her new freedom from housework when Martha simply disappeared. After a full week of devoting every spare minute to the chase, Suzy finally reached her on the phone.

"Martha, I've been so worried," Suzy began. "Have you been sick—or hurt?"

"No, I'm just fine," Martha answered.

"But, then, why didn't you come—or at least call? Is it something that we did?"

"Oh, no. It's just I decided to go back to what I was doing before."

"But, Martha," Suzy wailed. "You told me you weren't doing anything before."

"Yep, that's right. But then my car conked out. Had to work till I could get another one. Now I'm all set."

Suzy hung up in dismay and determined to select more carefully the next time. She consulted a reliable agency. Their first candidate was a tall, slim, tight-lipped blond. Remembering her own job interviews, Suzy made Jane comfortable and began a series of questions.

"Tell me about yourself, Jane. What do you like?"

"I like $3 an hour plus room and board. I expect my own room with a decent mattress, comfortable chair, and a color tv. Won't eat anything with artificial additives or preservatives in it. Saturdays, Sundays, and holidays are off. Also Thursday afternoons. If you're not on a bus line, I'll need to use the car. No heavy lifting, no diapers, and I don't do windows. Do you have other help?"

So much for Suzy's interviewing technique. She forgot the rest of her questions, and the session ended abruptly.

Anxious as she was to replace Martha, Suzy had to postpone the next interviews the agency had lined up because of Oak Hill. Oak Hill was John's first listing. He couldn't have been prouder if he'd brought home the Pulitzer Prize. The house belonged to John's boss.

"You've been there, Suzy." he said. "The Andersons bought it about 12 years ago to use as a weekend place. They keep their horses out there."

"Sure, I remember. Big old farmhouse, miles from town, up in the north hills."

"That's it. They have acreage and a view clear into the next county. Part of the house is over 100 years old. It's been added onto five or six times. Andy hasn't ever counted the rooms, but he guesses there are about 14."

"A monster to keep up, and expensive, too," Suzy was thinking. "A real woman-killer."

"Andy hates to let it go, but they don't get up there often enough to warrant the upkeep," John went on as if reading Suzy's mind.

"Mmmmm. The price seems high, John. Did you find any comparables?"

"Are you kidding? This place is one of a kind. Somebody's going to fall madly in love with it. Price'll be no object. I know you can find a buyer, Suzy."

Suzy was touched by John's confidence but half convinced he should have stuck to road equipment. They planned to hold an open house together on the following Sunday. As it happened, Erin woke up with a fever. A few dozen frantic phone calls failed to produce a responsible sitter, and Suzy couldn't find an available salesperson either. So, as it turned out, John stayed home with Erin, and Suzy took the boys with her to Oak Hill. They didn't mind, though; they were delighted with the prospect of a day in the country. Joey ecstatically collected jars for pollywogs and practiced with an old butterfly net he found, while Mike packed sandwiches for their lunch and carrots for the horses.

The viewer traffic was surprisingly heavy. Before the afternoon was half over, Suzy had to call Mike in to help her steer people through the maze of hallways and stairways. He did it very well and even seemed to be enjoying himself.

"Did you sell it, mom?" he asked eagerly after the last looker had finally gone.

"Not likely, hon," she replied. "This gang was mostly curious neighbors and tire kickers. Thanks a million for the help—couldn't have done it without you."

"Yeah, it's a big job. Do you believe I caught that one sicko trying to unscrew a hinge from a cupboard?"

"I believe it," Suzy sighed. "Let's get Joey and head home. I'm really bushed."

"I'll bet. You handle 'em really great, though, mom. Never lose your cool."

"We need just the right buyer," Suzy mused. "Someone who likes old things and high places. . . ."

"And hide-and-go-seek," Mike added.

During the week that followed, Erin recovered, and Suzy devoted most of her time to showing Oak Hill. John even showed it twice himself. However, his first group wouldn't even get out of the car to go look inside.

"Just wanted a free, chauffeur-driven ride in the country," he grumbled.

After the second tour, he was even more frustrated.

"Thought I had 'em," he told them at dinner. "We spent hours there. Then the idiot decided that the property taxes would triple in the next year or so."

"Well, you can't argue about a thing like that, John . . . " Suzy started to explain.

"I sure as hell can, and I did. I know a thing or two about taxes. He just wouldn't listen. Someday he'll be crying in his beer. Should have bought that baby when he had the chance."

"The agency sent another housekeeper," Suzy remarked, to change the subject. "She seems like a hard worker. She'd been working at the county hospital, and they say she was impeccable. She starts tomorrow."

"Did you ask if she could cook?" John asked. "Hospitals have a way of making everything taste like brussels sprouts."

"Ugh!" Joey and Erin said in unison.

Loretta did indeed keep the house clean—enough to satisfy the most demanding top sargeant. She sterilized doorknobs. She scrutinized guests, following the smokers around with an ashtray, sniffing her disapproval each time they flicked. Even the family was not immune. The children rebelled at being sent to the shower four and five times a day. Suzy herself was tongue-lashed for entering the kitchen with a dab of mud on one shoe. Loretta, Suzy decided, wasn't worth sacrificing one's God-given right to eat potato chips in the living room.

Loretta was succeeded by Cathy, who cooked reasonably well and kept the cleaning down to a bare minimum. Cathy was a sweet young thing, and the kids adored her. Suzy was free again to attack Oak Hill with new vigor, new ads, and, if necessary, good luck charms, voodoo, and holy water. She held another open house and once again took Mike along to help. That was the day he broke his ankle jumping over a farmer's fence. Mike never did explain whether that episode had to do with stolen fruit or an angry cow. But the open house was abruptly canceled in favor of a fast trip to the hospital.

Mike had to stay home for a week, but with Cathy's help, Suzy was able to continue her search for a buyer enamored of heights, horses, and hide-'n-seek. The buyers were good at hiding.

"It's a jinx, John," she said one night. "Can't you get the Andersons to drop the price?"

"Not without feeling like a damned fool," he replied.

"What do shepherds wear, John?" Suzy asked wearily.

"How do I know—sheepskins? What's that got to do with Oak Hill?"

"Nothing. It's got to do with Erin. She has a part in the school pageant and needs a costume."

"Pretty ridiculous, if you ask me," said John, annoyed. "You mothers let teachers get the best of you. Is this the same dingbat who's always asking for baby food jars?"

"Mmmm hmmm," Suzy nodded.

"Did you tell her we don't have any babies? Or are you going to have another just to please her?"

"Marjorie keeps me well supplied with jars," Suzy answered. "Don't hassle me, John. I'm intimidated by teachers. I've always been afraid they might send me to the cloakroom. Besides, I'd hate to be the cause of Erin's becoming a third grade dropout."

"Last month she told Erin to bring four empty paper towel rollers," John rattled on. "I'll bet we still have a closet full of unrestrained paper towels."

"We do," Suzy yawned. Before she could say anything else, they were interrupted by a plaintive call from above.

"Mo—om!"

"Be right up," Suzy called. "'Scuse me, hon. I promised to stop in on Mike before I conk out."

It had been a long time since Mike needed someone to come by and tuck him in. Suzy was proud of the boy, but conscious of the generation gap widening and the increasingly strained lines of communication developing between parent and offspring. Her conversations with him were more like a steady stream of trite commands: eat your vegetables; you aren't going to wear that, are you?; wash your hands; be home early; pick up your dirty clothes. No wonder he kept one ear glued to the phone and the other tuned to his radio, which blared forth at the decibel level of an air raid alert in an anvil factory.

"Hi, chum," she shouted above the din as she entered his room. "Isn't the gimp leg enough? Are you bucking for deafness too?"

"Hi, superstar," he replied, condescending to turn off Earth, Wind and Fire. "Sorry I'm all out of Perry Como. How's it going with Oak Hill?"

"Just between us two, I wish it'd burn down," Suzy whispered.

Mike laughed. "It'll sell, mom. It's a righteous house."

"What did you want to talk to me about?" Suzy asked.

"Oh—well—it's about Cathy."

"Cathy? You like her, don't you, Mike? Erin and Joey are wild about her. I don't know what I'd do with you laid up and no help."

"I know the kids like her, mom, but she's not good for them."

Suzy was startled. "What do you mean—too much candy?"

"More than that," Mike said rather reluctantly.

Suzy sighed, "Well, you'd better tell me."

"Last night she let them stay up and watch "Soap." She lets them take puffs on her cigarettes and gives them swigs of her beer. And have you seen her friends? Motorcycle guys with boots and black leather jackets. They use words that'd curl your hair."

"So that's where Joey heard that," Suzy began. "Thanks, Mike. I'm glad you told me."

Sweet little Cathy and friends were unceremoniously dismissed. Suzy was by now sufficiently discouraged to ask mother for help, which is to say, very downhearted indeed.

"Since I can't imagine a mother entrusting her precious children to hired help, I really don't know how I can be of any assistance," mother said pompously.

"That isn't quite fair, mother," Suzy replied. "Your parents always had live-in help when you were growing up."

"I try to reserve meaningful time with the family."

"My parents took in poor immigrant girls out of the kindness of their hearts."

"Kindness, my eye," Suzy snorted. "Worked them 16 hours a day, 7 days a week, and probably paid them a lousy $5 every Saturday. I don't think grandmother ever boiled an egg in her life."

Mother was visibly annoyed. "Suzy, I'm trying to tell you. Those live-in girls were not of good class. They were addicted to movie magazines and forever running off to meet the grocery boy behind the carriage house. Mama often remarked that she'd rather do the work herself, but, of course, you know how delicate she was. Papa wouldn't hear of her working in the kitchen. But she was always at home. She devoted herself tirelessly to seeing that we children weren't corrupted."

"It must be fun to be delicate," Suzy decided. She also wondered if mother wouldn't have benefited from a smattering of corruption. But mostly, Suzy thought, she'd gladly settle for an old-fashioned chore girl, even at the expense of keeping her supplied with movie magazines and grocery boys.

"If you must have help," mother droned on, "be sure to insist that they wear a proper uniform, use the basement facilities, and are trained to say 'Yes, ma'am' and 'No, ma'am' when spoken to."

The ultimate solution was pretty far from what mother had in mind. Genevieve was referred by one of Suzy's clients who was moving away. She came to the house to interview wearing shapeless slacks topped by a Chicago Bears sweatshirt. From the size of her, she might well have played for the Bears. Suzy and Genevieve were just sitting down to talk when Erin burst into the room demanding to know if her shepherd's costume was ready.

"Oh lord, I forgot about that! Is it tomorrow that you need it?" Suzy cried.

The phone rang, and Suzy had to excuse herself. There ensued a long wrangle with a buyer who was upset because the VA appraisal had come in $10,000 under the price he'd agreed to pay. When she finally finished and turned back to Erin and Genevieve, she was astonished to find herself facing a small shepherd.

"Nothing to it," Genevieve said diffidently. "We found a crooked stick in the yard, and I took a sheet from the closet."

Genevieve, it turned out, was the answer to a mother's prayer: another mother. She'd already raised eight kids of her own and gathered Suzy's brood to her ample bosom with unrestrained love. She could find lost library books, fix zippers, cook a quiche, make necklaces out of been can tabs, and create entrancing gingerbread men. She also taught Mike how to throw a knuckle ball. Genevieve became a member of the family—indivisible and indispensible.

Having (again) solved her domestic woes, Suzy could once more concentrate on the Oak Hill problem. Surprisingly enough, it was Mike who found the solution.

"Angora goats," he shouted excitedly one evening as Suzy walked in the door. "Ever hear of a guy raising goats?"

"Not lately," Suzy replied. "Anyone we know?"

"My English teacher's uncle. Name's Pruitt. He's moving here soon, and he's looking for a place where he can keep his goats. I told her about Oak Hill, and she just called. They'd like to see it tomorrow."

"Wow, fantastic!" Suzy exclaimed. "Wait a minute—not so fantastic."

"What's the problem?"

"Joey's the problem. Visiting Parents' Day's the problem. Each week a mother comes to class to do some special project with the kids, and tomorrow's my day."

"We can't postpone it, mom. They're only in town for a quick trip. Can't Joey's teacher do her own playdough thing?"

"It's important to Joey, Mike. The mothers compete like mad, and it makes the kids so proud. Maybe dad can skip out of work and take the showing. We'll ask him when he gets home," Suzy decided. Mike looked rather dubious.

The playdough versus Oak Hill conflict was duly laid on John's lap against a noisy background. Joey had overheard the discussion and lapsed into premature tears. John didn't see any reason why he couldn't take the showing.

"Dad," said Mike, phrasing his words carefully, "Mr. Pruitt's *my* prospect."

"I know, son. Mother and I really appreciate your help. If he buys, you'll get your reward," he said, misreading Mike's motive.

"No offense, dad, but mom's a real pro—I've watched her. Don't we Soldsines always throw in the first team? Any damn fool can make playdough."

Suzy held her breath, but John laughed. "Gotcha, Mike. Mother can take the Pruitts, and I'll be the damn fool."

John's appearance at the Happy Hollow School was memorable. He pleaded an allergy to playdough. Also to finger paints and all other forms of artsy-craftsy activities. Instead, he elected to make flapjacks. The children helped stir the batter and shouted ecstatically as he flipped the cakes high in the air. The teacher didn't even complain when one half-cooked stack missed the pan and splattered on her desk. It was a triumph. Joey was in his glory. The other Happy Hollow mothers were green with envy. The other fathers never forgave John his earth-shattering break with precedent.

Meanwhile, Suzy drove the Pruitts to Oak Hill with a mind full of doubts and a heart full of prayers. The Pruitts were an elderly, childless couple, moving to town to be near their niece. They were a taciturn pair, but they both glowed like neon signs when the conversation turned to goats. During the ride out, Suzy learned the name, personality, and history of every one of their 20 animals. They said it was just a hobby, but Suzy could see it was much more than that.

The first things they looked at upon reaching Oak Hill were the stable and pasture. Mr. Pruitt scooped up a clump of earth and fell in love. He was ready to buy. But after Mrs. Pruitt had gone through the cumbersome house she was far from convinced. Suzy did the only thing a salesperson can do under those circumstances: she sat them down at the kitchen table with a pitcher of cold spring water and disappeared while they wrangled. They bought.

The offer was far short of the asking price. But Suzy met with the Andersons later, and it was accepted. John was estatic. They decided to take the whole family, including Genevieve, out for a celebration dinner.

"It's thanks to you, Mike," Suzy said at dinner. "You pulled it all off."

"Do I get a commission?" he asked eagerly.

"It's illegal to share commissions with an unlicensed person, young man," John teased. "But you're up for a handsome gift."

"A stereo, maybe?"

"Why not?"

"With woofers and tweeters?"

"Sure," John replied cautiously. "Whatever they are."

It was a glorious evening. John and Suzy hugged a lot. Erin ate a banana split. Joey fell asleep in his plate. Genevieve flirted with the bouncer. Mike dreamed about his stereo and wondered if he could dig up enough prospects to merit a Corvette by the time he was 16.

READER'S QUIZ

This is a guaranteed foolproof quiz. All answers are correct. Give yourself a mark of 100, and brag a lot.

1. As a mother with a career, I'm eternally grateful for

    _____ a.   "Sesame Street."
    _____ b.   frozen food.
    _____ c.   nursery schools.
    _____ d.   the Pill.
    _____ e.   other

2. When a mother says "Ask your father" she knows the answer he gives will be

    _____ a.   no.
    _____ b.   "Hell, no."
    _____ c.   "Over my dead body."
    _____ d.   "Ask your mother."
    _____ e.   other

3. Domestic help can best be described as

    _____ a.   unobtainable.
    _____ b.   unaffordable.
    _____ c.   unreliable.
    _____ d.   unbelievable.
    _____ e.   other

4. I knew my son was emerging into adolescence when

    _____ a.   he started taking the phone into the coat closet and
               shutting the door.
    _____ b.   he nearly bled to death after his first attempt at shaving.
    _____ c.   he started calling me "shorty."
    _____ d.   he took down his Snoopy posters and put up Dolly Parton.
    _____ e.   other

5. The listing I remember with the least pleasure is the one that

    _____ a.   should have been condemned.
    _____ b.   housed 27 cats.
    _____ c.   had 57 steps between streets and front door.
    _____ d.   never sold.
    _____ e.   other

11
All Hail the Bottom Line

Although the tug-of-war between office and domestic duties would never be totally resolved, Suzy's real estate career continued an unqualified success. She had equaled her first year's earnings before her second year with FFC was half over. While Helga was still the company's top producer, Suzy had forged her way into second place over Harry, who bore her no malice. (Harry had reached his comfort zone and was content to stay there.) Clara's consistent ability to list had lifted her to a position close behind Harry, and Frances's energy and enthusiasm were bringing her into strong contention. There were other lesser lights and a stream of transients on the way in or out. Hubert nursed them in, and Buster escorted them out with tiresome regularity.

Mr. Foley disappeared from the scene for 2 full months and returned to the company and the country club looking incredibly young and healthy. Opinion was divided as to whether he'd visited a health farm or had his face lifted—or both. Mr. Feinberg had grunted his satisfaction when Crystal Cliff sold out and now devoted himself to completing construction. Mr. Chong continued to keep a watchful eye on Mrs. Niggardly, the petty cash, and the coffee grounds. This was the company pecking order when Buster announced a gigantic sales contest.

"For 60 days, gang," he trumped to the sales staff, "we'll divide you into two teams. Suzy and Harry will captain one group. Helga, you and Clara have the other. The rest will be chosen by lot. The winning team is the one producing the biggest dollar volume."

"And what's the prize," asked Helga, "Acapulco again?"

Buster winced. "Nothing like that. This is strictly for fun. The winners'll ride in chauffeur-driven limousines to a gala dinner of filet mignon and champagne. The losers will come on the bus, eat beans, and wash the dishes."

"Think I'll take 2 months off," Frances whispered when she found she'd been attached to Helga's team. "Poverty would be a small price to pay for seeing that old bat wash dishes."

"I can't afford that luxury," Clara replied. "What's the point of all this childish horseplay? Aren't we supposed to be independent contractors, doing business as we see fit? I don't understand."

Harry laughed out loud. "Clara, you're forgetting that 45 cents out of every dollar you bring in goes into the company coffers. It's your money that Chong doles out so grudgingly, and he's making damned sure that a sizable portion of it winds up in his *profit* box. His profit, not yours."

"So, if the profit's slipping, let old Chong eat beans," Frances cried irreverently.

"Expense is only half the battle," Harry explained, chewing his pipe stem. "Profit's the difference between income and expense. When the income declines, Buster has to get out his whip."

"So this is calculated to make us work harder?" Frances asked innocently.

"Of course," Harry replied. "It's the oldest kind of motivation going. Love of winning versus fear of failing, with a dash of for-the-good-of-the-team thrown in."

"Pitting us against each other, possibly even destroying friendships," Clara began.

"Hey, wait a minute," Suzy said, having listened with growing concern. "You're taking it too seriously. This is for laughs, and it might even do us some good. I know I've been feeling a touch complacent lately. Not pushing quite as hard as I can. Maybe we all need a kick in the buns."

"You, complacent?" they all shouted.

"You know what I mean," Suzy went on. "When it starts coming easy, some of the thrill is gone. The contest is kind of silly, but it's a reason to get into high gear again. I intend to win, but I won't lose friends over it. Happens I like beans."

"Wait till they start beating the drums," Harry warned. "It's calculated to make us all mortal enemies."

Later, Suzy and Harry shared a cup of coffee. "Harry," she asked impulsively, "have you ever thought about going into business for yourself?"

"Not only thought of it but did it. That was 10 years ago. Want to see my scars?"

"It didn't work out?"

"With a flawless sense of timing, I opened the doors at one of those marvelous moments when the lenders ran out of money and the buyers keeled over and played dead."

"But if you'd hung on."

"Hanging's what I did, all right," Harry chuckled. "By the time the sheriff helped me close the door, I was minus my investment and $10,000 in debt."

"Would you do it again?" Suzy asked.

"No," Harry answered firmly, "I put that pocketful of dreams to rest. Would you?"

"Oh, Lord, I'm far from the point of even thinking about it," Suzy replied. "But I am feeling kind of restless—like I need a new challenge."

Suzy had challenge enough on her hands when Hubert and Buster did, as predicted, begin to beat the drums for the contest. There were posters, pep talks, and daily tallies. With a few exceptions, the agents responded by reaching the level of enthusiasm they usually felt for a lecture on existentialism or a greasy hamburger at Dino's. In other words, their rate of achievement was, as always, related to their degree of hunger. As the deadline approached, the teams were neck and neck, and the tension grew.

It was during the contest that Joel approached Suzy for help with a new listing he'd acquired.

"This'll make some deserving investor delirious with joy," he said. "It's an old building but well built and sitting smack in the path of progress. With 4,000 square feet of commercial space and nine offices with solid tenants—at one million, three, it shows a return of . . ."

"Whoa!" Suzy shouted. "Investors just aren't in my league, Joel. They're not people."

"Of course they are," Joel cried. "They're the same people you sell those fancy houses to, Suzy baby, and you're too good to settle for that. It's time you broke into the big time."

"I'm confident with houses, Joel," Suzy explained. I'm on my clients' wavelength. They're not looking for lumber and bricks but for convenience, privacy, or status. They fall in love with things like apple trees, attics, vestibules, and views. Meet their emotional needs and the money's a cinch. But investors—they babble about taxes and cash flows. I feel like I'm in a shooting gallery, and I'm the sitting duck."

"It's the same people, though," Joel argued. "Different motivations but not necessarily unemotional. Investors are basically after four things: income, tax shelters, appreciation, or a monument."

"Monument?" Suzy asked. "Maybe they should be shopping in the cemetery."

Joel laughed. "That's where the monument buyer usually winds up. He's on an ego trip. Wants to point to a big hunk of masonry and say 'it's *mine*'—name on the cornerstone and all that garbage."

"Like buying a fancy address with a house thrown in?"

"Exactly," Joel replied. "Take a look at it, Suzy. This building's no monument—it's a winner all the way."

But Suzy had to put Joel's building out of mind as the contest roared to a close. Her team was working hard but trailed in the stretch by one or two commissions.

"Helga's pulling dirty tricks, Harry," Suzy stormed in one morning. "My phone messages are disappearing before I get 'em, and yesterday at my open house, one of her agents was intercepting clients out on the street and steering them down the block to her listing!"

"Didn't you expect that?" he asked mildly.

"What'll we do—complain to Buster or beat her at her own game?"

"Better still, let's lock her in the john for about 8 days," Harry suggested.

"How about a black widow in her message box?" Joel proposed.

Suzy laughed, "And I'm the one who said we'd keep it light and lively."

Suzy's team racked up five more transactions in the final days. Helga's group had six. Despite her vows, Suzy burst into tears when she learned that her team had lost.

"It was a rip-off," she told John later. "I hope her filet's tough and her champagne's flat."

"Nice guys don't always finish last, honey," John said soothingly. "You'll have your day with Helga."

"Damned right I will. Wait till the next awards banquet," Suzy cried. "I'll win if I have to sell city hall."

The steak-and-champagne eaters enjoyed the banquet and their well-earned hangovers. The crow-eaters were good sports and returned to work with a vengeance. City hall wasn't for sale, so Suzy asked Joel for packets of information about his commercial building and mailed them to eight of her clients. One of them responded with a request for more data. Ed Schubert was a car dealer who'd both bought and sold homes through Suzy. He sounded surprised when she called to ask if he'd like to see the building. He politely declined.

"Good Lord," Suzy exclaimed to John, "how can people spend millions of dollars without even wanting to see what they're buying?"

"What they buy is the bottom line," John said patiently. "He's probably familiar with the building, and it wouldn't matter if he weren't, just as long as it looks like a good place to plant his money."

"OK," said Suzy, hauling out reams of Joel's computer printouts, "just point me to the bottom line. I need help, John. I was hoping Ed might fall in love with the little gargoyles over the entrance. Obviously, that isn't the way to go."

John pored over the papers and reduced them to a simple, believable statement, explaining it to Suzy as he went along. Neither the rental income nor the tax write-offs seemed to justify the asking price. Suzy was discouraged.

"Haven't finished yet," John mumbled. "Let's look at Joel's projections. The location's terrific, and that means the value of the land will be going up like a rocket in the next 10 years. The land alone may be worth the price."

"Glad to know we're still selling real estate and not numbers," Suzy yawned.

It wasn't 'till Erin woke up with a bad dream that they realized they'd been at it for more than 4 hours. John now felt that they were ready to talk to the clients, and Suzy felt too tired to care.

They met with Ed Schubert the following day. Ed was a salesman himself and had a talent for answering questions with questions. He studied John's statements intently.

"What do you think of it, Ed?" Suzy asked enthusiastically. "Isn't the location great?"

"Not bad. Can the income be increased?"

"Joel feels it can. I haven't studied the tenant leases yet," John replied.

"It's got scads of parking," Suzy added.

"Mmmm hmm, but you'd lose a lot if they widened that street. Is that a possibility?" Ed asked.

"I'd have to check with the planning commission," John answered, making another note on his pad.

"Everyone says the building's in perfect condition," Suzy said. "You wouldn't have to spend a bundle fixing it up."

"Well, if rents are going to go up, we'll have to put in central air. Got any figures on that?"

"I'll get some," John replied.

"It's bound to go up in value. Don't you think so, Ed?" Suzy asked.

"It might. Have any others I can look at for comparison?"

The conversational ball stayed in the air for better than an hour, with Suzy probing, Ed countering, and John scribbling.

"We're a wonderful team," Suzy said afterwards. Do you think he's interested? I couldn't seem to move in for a close."

"Too soon," John replied. "He won't make a play 'till he's seen all the cards."

Uncovering all the cards took an agonizing succession of weeks. Ultimately, Suzy was taken by surprise when Ed called one day and asked her to write up an offer at $1.1 million. At Ed's office, Suzy pulled out the same offer form she used for residential sales, kicking herself for not having asked if it were appropriate and wondering if there'd be room for all the zeros. Ed didn't seem to notice. He told Suzy to make the offer for cash and casually penned his name to an earnest money check for $25,000. Suzy made her way back to the office and arrived in one piece despite two traffic tickets, one for speeding and one for running a red light.

"I've got it, Joel," she shrieked. "A cash offer for $1.1 million. Only, I think I used the wrong form."

"Baby, if the offer's good, I couldn't care if you scratched it on modeling clay with a picnic fork. The price sounds right, but I'm not sure about the terms."

"You're kidding, Joel. It's for cash. What could be sweeter?"

"Cash won't buy my seller out of a walloping capital gains tax. We're going to have to work out an exchange, baby. But don't worry about it. We have an apartment house in mind. Trouble is, the apartment house owner wants an exchange, too."

Investors have varying motivations.

"Sounds like you're going to set up a chain of dominoes," Suzy said dejectedly. "How long does this go on?"

"Patience, lady, and keep the faith. I'll work it out," Joel said reassuringly.

Suzy kept the faith. She got daily reports as Joel put Plan A into operation. It was to be a triple exchange, with Ed buying a warehouse, then trading it for the apartment building, then for the commercial building. Before that could all be assembled, the warehouse burned down. Joel then tried the exchange with another commercial building, but the apartment owner's tax attorney didn't like that one. Plan C involved leaving the apartment house owner out of it and just trading one commercial building for the other. That could have worked if the second building's owner hadn't gone into bankruptcy.

Mr. Feinberg was called in to help with Plans D and E. Suzy kept John and Ed informed, but as months went by she got caught up in her residential work and gradually lost interest. The awards banquet was coming up. In deference to Helga's disenchantment with Mexico, the company had decided to give the top producer a new car. Helga was still in the lead but not by much.

"I'll give you my prospects, Suzy, if it'll help. I mean it," Frances offered. "Helga doesn't deserve a car after the stuff she pulled in the contest. I wouldn't give her a leaky laundry tub."

"How about a year's supply of Maalox?" Harry suggested affably.

"Or a gold-plated battle-ax," Clara added.

"I'd vote for cyanide," Frances laughed.

"You turkeys by any chance talking about awards?" Joel asked, coming into the group. "Who's in the lead?"

"Helga, of course. We're trying to think up a way to spike her guns," Frances replied.

"Would $20,000 in the Suzy column help?" Joel asked blandly.

"Joel, you don't mean . . ." Suzy cried.

"I do, baby. Your Mr. Schubert has bought himself a building. Set to close next week."

"Did you work out a tax-free exchange for your sellers?"

"We sure as hell hope so. I can't swear it'll qualify, but old Feinberg's put together such a devious deal that it may take the IRS 20 years to figure it out. Meanwhile, you and I live in the lap of luxury."

"It puts you on top, Suzy," Harry said after some quick calculations. "And Joel will take second. Helga'll have to settle for third."

"Hold it," Suzy said. "Half of this commission is John's. I never could have done it alone."

"Nuts to that," Frances shouted. "He won't mind, and we won't tell."

John was properly thrilled. "Watching Helga lose is worth any sacrifice," he stated gallantly. "This'll be a banquet to remember."

"And you'll rent a tux without a whimper," Suzy laughed.

"Won't have to," he replied. "I've bought one. Just make sure you turn over the check, so I can pay for it. And don't get any wild ideas 'till I've stashed away some tax money."

John enjoyed the banquet to the hilt. He even made favorable comments about the food. Suzy got a standing ovation from her pals and couldn't say anything intelligent. Helga was unable to be present, due to a sudden illness.

"John, I should have thanked all the people who've helped me," Suzy whispered later.

"Glad you didn't," he laughed. "I've always wondered why the Academy Award winners can't see what a bore it is. By the way, what new extravagance are you cooking up—two-piano duets?"

"You get an *A* for mind reading," Suzy smiled. "I was having an expensive thought. Not just for me, though, but for the whole Soldsine team."

"How about a trust fund for the children's education?" John suggested.

"How about Europe?"

"I have a sinking feeling you're going to tell me it's motivational," he groaned.

"No—just fun. We'll take the kids and spend 3 or 4 weeks. See all the places we've read about."

"They're pretty young for Europe," John ventured.

"They're just right. Old enough to enjoy it and not quite to the point where they wouldn't be caught dead traveling with parents. Mike's already borderline. Would June be OK or would you prefer July?"

John doubted if he could take the time off—but he did. Mother hinted that she could be persuaded to come along—but she wasn't. Suzy knew she could trust Genevieve to hold down the house, and her friends to keep her clients happy and out of Helga's greedy hands.

The trip was glorious. John took rolls and rolls of film while the kids bought out the souvenir shops. Suzy talked to strangers and hit upon a couple from home who happened to be planning to sell their house and buy another when they returned. It was an unqualified success.

READER'S QUIZ

This is a guaranteed foolproof quiz. All answers are correct. Give yourself a mark of 100, and brag a lot.

1. Sales contests can be compared to

    _____ a.   the brass ring on the merry-go-round.
    _____ b.   the plastic frog in a box of Cracker Jacks.
    _____ c.   a carrot on a stick.
    _____ d.   a cattle prod.
    _____ e.   other

2. Losing a contest might inspire an agent to

    _____ a.   do better.
    _____ b.   quit.
    _____ c.   change the rules.
    _____ d.   murder the winner.
    _____ e.   other

3. My definition of *bottom line* is

    _____ a.   my son's semester grades.
    _____ b.   the graphic projection of my recent slump.
    _____ c.   the depth table on my swimming pool.
    _____ d.   the ridge my bikini pants make under tight slacks.
    _____ e.   other

4. Investor clients are

    _____ a.   calculating and cool.
    _____ b.   demanding and devious.
    _____ c.   wealthy and whimsical.
    _____ d.   royal and reckless.
    _____ e.   other

5. A very large commission often leads to

    _____ a.   a higher tax bracket.
    _____ b.   a faster car.
    _____ c.   a big head.
    _____ d.   divorce.
    _____ e.   other

12
Going for Broker

When Suzy returned from abroad, the office was buzzing with headline news. Mr. Foley had announced the company's plans for opening a branch office in the new Westwood shopping center, in the midst of a rapidly growing medium-to-high-priced residential area. Buster had offered Helga the job of managing the new office. While supposedly thinking this over, Helga had leased office space next door to FFC's proposed location, formed her own corporation, and then tendered her resignation.

"Was Buster furious?" Suzy asked Harry.

"You couldn't prove it, Harry replied, chewing on his pipe stem. "He's been Mr. Sweetness-and-Light—insisting that nobody's indispensible and telling us all to wish her lotsa luck. We're even planning a small farewell party on Friday. I'm in charge of collecting for her parting gift. At the present rate of generosity, it'll probably be a pencil box or calendar."

"I'll donate," Suzy volunteered. "I feel kind of responsible for her leaving."

"Because you beat her out? Nonsense."

"She never has liked me, Harry. You know that."

"Maybe not," Harry replied. "But Helga's a reformed woman now. Being positively charming to all of us—and in direct proportion to our earnings."

"You don't mean she'd try to persuade us to join her, do you? That's unethical!"

"It might just cross her mind," Harry laughed. "You can bet we're all in Buster's prayers these days, along with the unholy hope that Helga'll go bankrupt and/or break her scrawny neck."

"Who's slated to manage the new branch?" Suzy inquired. "And do we get a choice about working there?"

"We breathlessly await the word. So far, the powers that be haven't leaked a clue. Best guess is that Hubert will get the job temporarily. He's upped his dosage of pep pills."

The party for Helga was less than memorable. The wine was cheap and the chips soggy. Everyone said the right things with just about the degree of warmth one would expect to find at a wake for a loan collector. Helga rewarded Buster's hospitality by buttonholing the top agents and offering a higher commission split than FFC was paying. Strangely enough, she got no takers.

Suzy was relieved when Helga left. As is always the case, her 3 weeks' vacation left her feeling as if she needed at least 2 more. Her mail and messages were piled higher than usual. And Buster had assigned her another understudy to "polish," as he put it. Brad was a scrawny young man with an abrasive manner and bad skin. He was also Mrs. Foley's nephew. Suzy felt that Brad's rough edges were more in need of a chisel than a buff. She was struggling with him one morning, trying to explain that a cheery "hello" is a better way to answer the phone than simply picking it up and barking "yup," when Frances breezed in.

"Suzy, I hope I'm not interrupting," she said, plopping her papers down on the desk. "The sale I made in Mercer Woods is all screwed up. The seller had a survey made last spring, but the damned buyer insisted on a new survey, and it's not the same. There's this fence, you see, and now we don't know whose fence it is, or whose land it's on, and everybody's in a total tizz. What'll I do?"

"How about handing the whole damned thing to Buster. He's paid to manage this zoo," Suzy replied abruptly.

Frances looked hurt and contrite. "Gosh, I'm sorry," she cried. "It just seems so natural to come to you because you got me started on the right track, and you're so good at finding ways of solving these problems. Buster makes me feel like a cop's handing me a speeding ticket. You should be a manager, Suzy. Have you thought of asking for the new office?"

"No one's mentioned it to me," Suzy answered evasively. "Forgive the nasty disposition, Frances—I didn't mean to snap at you like that. It's just that all the people I work with wind up using me for a combination troubleshooter and Mother Confessor."

"The resident Ann Landers," Frances giggled. "I'll get you one of those reversible signs: 'Doctor is in,' 'Doctor is out,' like Lucy uses in 'Peanuts.' Maybe you should have a light on your desk like the priest's confessional."

"About the fence," said Suzy, trying valiantly to get Frances back to business. "Notify both companies that you're going to have a third survey made, and that you'll expect them to pay for it. They probably won't, so you'd better have Mrs. Niggardly's OK."

"Oh, thanks, Suzy. I knew you'd come through," said Frances as she grabbed her papers and darted off.

Within a week, Europe was a dim memory. Suzy was listing and selling at her old level and even had another investor transaction in the embryonic stages. Brad was neither very interesting nor promising, but he was useful. Suzy kept him busy delivering documents, feeding parking meters, and filling her coffee cup.

Suzy and Clara proudly signed up for the last of their Graduate, Realtors® Institute courses offered by the local Board of Realtors®. It was the third in a series of week-long seminars that battered their brains with a mind-boggling array of miscellaneous information and left their fannies as numb as their minds. Although she was not entirely sure why she needed to know how to turn an apartment house into a condominium, Suzy enjoyed the stimulus. She noted with pride that her fellow students were among the best in the business.

"If I earn the right to put that precious GRI after my name," Suzy told John, "I'll owe it all to my ironclad panty girdle."

"I must say, your latent passion for education amazes me," John replied. "What does it get you—ribbons on your chest? Do your clients even know what the letters stand for?"

"Far as your average guy's concerned, GRI could stand for 'going rapidly insane,'" Suzy chuckled.

"Does the course relate to selling?"

"It's a little bit about a lot of things," Suzy replied. "Clara says all we've learned is how much we don't know yet."

"Sounds like an endless process. Where do you go from here?" John asked.

"I guess the next target for us professional students is the broker's exam," Suzy said offhandedly. "Clara and I are both eligible now."

John drummed his fingers on the table. "That means another course, I suppose, and a lot of studying at the expense of selling time. Not that I mind, Suzy, but I'm wondering if it's worthwhile. You don't need the broker's license unless you plan to manage an office. Is that what you have in mind?"

Suzy was beginning to feel uncomfortable and again wondered why the phone never rings when you want it to.

"I don't really know," she said slowly. "Just seems I've gotten into a rut and need some new goals. Working with new agents is a kick. I got more satisfaction out of Frances's first listing than I did from my own."

"Lord, what a glutton," John laughed. "Isn't being top producer satisfying enough? Doesn't $50,000 a year fulfill your ego needs? Reminds me of when Erin was born. The first thing you said was, 'Now that we have a boy and a girl, what's left to try for?'"

"Did I say that?" Suzy smiled. "Relax, John. I haven't been offered a managership, and I don't intend to run off like Helga did. You realize, though, that I already have managerial burdens and am getting precious little compensation for it."

"There's more to managing than telling Frances to order a survey or Brad to wear socks," John suggested.

The blessed phone finally rang, and Suzy trotted off to take another listing. As a matter of fact, Suzy and Clara had already signed up for their broker's course and had debated about breaking the news to Buster. In the wake of Helga's departure he might be feeling understandably sensitive. Since his signature was required on the application, Suzy finally mustered enough courage to seek an interview. Buster didn't seem overly perturbed. "I hope you don't expect the company to pay for the course," he began.

"Heavens, no. Wouldn't dream of causing an independent contractor problem."

"Right, and we don't offer any extra compensation to salespeople who are licensed as brokers. Frankly, I don't understand why you're bothering."

"That makes two of you," Suzy thought. "It's like Mount Everest," she suggested brightly. "You climb it because it's there. Besides, it'll give me a little extra prestige and a few more options."

"Prestige and a dime won't even get you a phone call anymore," Buster snorted. "As for options—what could be as lucrative as what you're already doing?"

"Well, Helga . . .''

"Helga's making the mistake of her life. She'll waste her time paying bills, ordering supplies, and making coffee and then wind up with half the income she had here."

"Maybe she knows that," Suzy mused. "I don't think Helga left for money. She wants to be somebody important."

Buster nodded agreement. "Yes, I can see that, but the salespeople *are* the important people in a real estate company. We managers are just a support system for the sales staff."

"So, how come you act like a boss?" Suzy thought.

"The dumbest thing a company can do is take top-notch salespeople out of selling and put 'em in management," Buster went on, "and 99 times out of 100 they make lousy managers. It's got to be a losing situation."

Suzy bit her lip. "There are some exceptions to that rule," she suggested.

If Buster knew of any, he apparently couldn't bring them to mind. He signed Suzy's license application without further comment.

The broker's course covered the same material that Suzy had previously studied, but in more depth. It shouldn't have been difficult if one remembered. Unfortunately, day-to-day real estate practice did little to reinforce knowledge that there are four (five? six?) warranties in a general warranty deed. Suzy found herself struggling to keep up.

"Relax, baby. It's a piece of cake," Eloise said blithely when they met for lunch. "What are you worrying for?"

"You'd worry too if the only study time you could find was sitting on the pot," Suzy laughed.

"So, arrange to be moderately constipated," Eloise suggested. "The reason I called, Suzy—is that I've nominated you for vice president of the Board of Realtors®."

She doesn't sell much, but she certainly is impressive.

"You've *what?*" Suzy exclaimed. "Forget it, Eloise. My life's complicated enough without politics."

"Well, we're not expecting you to stand on street corners shaking hands, dummy. You're a shoo-in. The opposition won't even get his own mother's vote. Just leave everything to me."   This, Suzy was more than happy to do.

Suzy and Clara discovered that taking a broker's course is a marvelous way to inspire all the clients one hasn't heard from in months to come forward and demand immediate service. They'd planned to attend the lectures together, but as things worked out they were lucky if one or the other made it.

While they were cramming, the Westwood branch opened its doors. As Harry had predicted, Hubert was appointed temporary manager in charge of frenzied fanfare. Suzy and Clara were both allowed to transfer to the new office. Harry and Frances stayed behind but dropped in often enough to keep in touch.

"Pretty plush digs," Harry remarked. "You kids look as comfortable as pigs in a mudhole."

"Has Helga stuck her nose in yet?" Frances asked.

"Of course," Suzy replied. "She's already appropriated every form we have—just blanks out the FFC logo and adds her own. She also uses our computer terminal because hers hasn't been delivered yet."

"I'm surprised Hubert'd let her do that," Frances cried.

"She waits until after he's left," Suzy laughed. "Hubert's driving us right up the wall."

"Your grand opening party was terrific," Harry said.

"We've had five of those," Suzy replied wearily. "Also sent mailers to everybody in town from accountants to xylophone players. I think my tongue's permanently glued to the roof of my mouth."

"Tell Hubert his biorhythms show a triple crisis. He'll run right home to bed fast enough," Harry suggested.

"I still think you ought to be the manager, Suzy," Frances chimed in. "You've got everything it takes."

"Well, Buster doesn't agree," Suzy replied lightly. "And judging from the way I'm flubbing the broker's course, he's looking righter all the time."

Suzy couldn't afford much time for chitchat. She continued to work with clients, work on Brad, and work at studying in odd moments. When exam time came—too fast and too soon—she suspected that she was still far from ready for it. After she skipped questions 1—11, her suspicion became a certainty. Nevertheless, she got through the test, making sufficient educated guesses to fan a faint and flickering spark of hope while she waited for the results. When the dire news arrived, Suzy experienced an overwhelming flood of disappointment. She'd failed.

Clara, on the other hand, passed. Suzy was genuinely happy about that, but she was in for another dose of disappointment when Buster announced Clara's appointment as manager of the new office. She congratulated Clara and then quickly called Eloise for a consolation drink.

"So you blew it—so what? I took the damned thing three times," Eloise said, pouring the wine.

"You didn't tell me that," Suzy exclaimed.

"My little secret. But now for the good news. You won the election, Suzy. It was a landslide. Didn't I tell you?"

"The election? Lord, I'd forgotten all about it. That's great—I think. Now why in hell didn't I think of having you take the broker's exam in my place?"

"How much did you miss by?" Eloise asked.

"*One* lousy question!"

"So, the next time you memorize one more lousy fact."

"Right," Suzy smiled. "I'll go again. You can bet your one and only Halston original on that. I mean to be a broker if I have to memorize the Old Testament in ancient Hebrew."

"Too bad they haven't been requiring that lately," Eloise remarked. "That test isn't the real problem, is it, Suzy? I have a feeling it's Clara getting the manager's job that's got you down."

"Nothing against Clara, but I wanted the job, and I thought I deserved a crack at it. You know how they feel about taking top salespeople into management."

"Oldest axiom in the business," Eloise said briskly. "Sharpshooters belong in the front lines. The executive suite is reserved for people who can chew out a secretary when she forgets to polish the mahogany desk and chair."

"But their first choice was Helga," Suzy said plaintively.

"Sure. That's the little known other half of the axiom. When a top producer gets the bug to be a manager, you'd better offer him the chance, or he'll quit. Helga undoubtedly threatened. Maybe Clara did, too. Did you?"

"No," Suzy said slowly. "I never even came right out and said I wanted the job."

"There you are, madam vice president. You now have the script in hand. First get the license, then ask for the job—and if you get turned down, threaten."

"Nothing to it," Suzy laughed. "'Scuse me while I go order some desk polish."

There was nothing to it. Suzy passed her broker's exam with flying colors on the next go-round. Meanwhile, FFC announced that a second branch office would be opening soon. Suzy asked Buster for the position and received in reply another long dissertation on the evils of salespeople aspiring to management.

"It isn't easy, Suzy. Look at the work you've put in on Brad, and he isn't making it," Buster ventured.

"Don't pull that stuff," Suzy cried. "One interview would've convinced me that Brad couldn't sell his own mother a cold drink on a hot day!"

"OK, so he wasn't interviewed, but . . ."

"Sorry, Buster," Suzy went on, "but I'm looking for a new challenge, and if you don't have anything to offer me, I'll just have to look elsewhere."

Eloise was right, as usual. Buster capitulated with good grace. It was announced at the next sales meeting that Realtor Suzy Soldsine, newly elected vice president of the Board of Realtors®, would manage the new Eastwood branch when it opened.

READER'S QUIZ

This is a guaranteed foolproof quiz. All answers are correct. Give yourself a mark of 100, and brag a lot.

1. When I return to the office after a vacation, I usually find

    _____ a.   that my desk has been appropriated.
    _____ b.   that my supplies have disappeared.
    _____ c.   that my job has been "reclassified."
    _____ d.   that my head aches.
    _____ e.   other

2. After being named salesperson of the year, one's next goal might be

    _____ a.   staying on top.
    _____ b.   taking up a new career.
    _____ c.   hiring a bodyguard.
    _____ d.   retirement.
    _____ e.   other

3. Salespeople aspire to take advanced courses in real estate so that they can

    _____ a.   impress their bosses.
    _____ b.   support their local real estate schools.
    _____ c.   get to know other people who are taking courses.
    _____ d.   acquire the right to wear ribbons on their name badges at conventions.
    _____ e.   other

4. Before taking the examination to become a broker, a salesperson usually must

   _____ a. find the time.
   _____ b. find the money.
   _____ c. find a good reason.
   _____ d. find someone who can explain closing statements.
   _____ e. other

5. In selecting a branch manager, a real estate company looks for

   _____ a. strength and fortitude.
   _____ b. charm and finesse.
   _____ c. a paperwork freak.
   _____ d. a willing body.
   _____ e. other

13
Move Over, Century 21

Suzy's ultimate decision to leave FFC didn't come on suddenly. Nor was it the direct result of either getting or not getting a crack at a managerial position right away. In fact, it didn't relate to any particular event in her own career, but rather, it came about because of some fairly momentous changes in the careers of three other people. It was, to put it simply, kismet.

Clara made a smooth ascension into management. In her youth, Clara had managed a truck-stop restaurant and had acquired considerable talent for getting things done under difficult and often impossible circumstances. She was courteous and capable with clients and tenderly supportive of troubled salespeople. On occasion, she could even terrorize a reluctant lender into humble acquiescence. She proved adept at scrounging those things Mr. Chong couldn't or wouldn't provide, ran a tight ship, and aged visibly under the strain.

If Suzy harbored any small green-eyed monster or a latent fear that the new relationship might affect their friendship, these were soon dispelled. The women's admiration and affection for each other was, if anything, increased.

"I think you're too damned good-natured," Suzy told her when they sat down together for a cup of coffee after an especially harrowing day. "You're wearing yourself out. Is it worthwhile?"

"Good question," Clara replied, mopping her forehead with a paper towel. "It's longer hours, more grief, and less compensation. But I knew that going in."

"Sure you did, and so do I," Suzy went on. "But we've asked for it, and now I'm wondering what for. Maybe we're selfless types, who get more jollies from helping someone else succeed than we get from our own triumphs. Are we bucking for sainthood or just overflowing with maternal instincts?"

Clara laughed. "Can't see myself in either role, can you?"

"An ego trip, then," Suzy pursued the subject. "Maybe it's the prestige—your own office cubicle with an outside window and your name on the door, your own secretary, a title. . . ."

"I gave up worrying about a title when I realized I'd never be May Queen," Clara replied. "Believe me, that so-called secretary Chong hired, who scratches her head all day and never learned the alphabet, is no great joy. Maybe it is some kind of ego trip, though. I wanted new worlds to conquer—to be a part of the decision-making process. I got tired of being told I was an independent contractor when in fact I was a damned puppet, with Foley, Feinberg, and Chong pulling the strings."

"So now you go to management meetings. Are you a string-puller?"

"Haven't caught hold of one yet," Clara replied. "I started out like the burning bush, full of big ideas; they were taken under advisement. I've requested certain things for my office; my requests were taken under advisement. I've ventured a few complaints. . . ."

"Let me guess. Taken under advisement?"

"I always knew you were a smart kid. I have all the responsibility for making this branch profitable. The allocation of overhead is unreal, and believe me, Suzy, I hear about every drop of red ink."

"But surely they've given you some authority."

"The authority's where it always was. I go downtown to talk to Mr. Foley about a television advertising campaign, and I wind up talking to Chong or Niggardly about why I requisitioned a new wastebasket without checking the garage sales for a secondhand one."

"You sound a bit disenchanted," Suzy said, getting up to pour some more coffee.

"Also disloyal," Clara laughed. "Did you know, Suzy, that managers are expected to overflow with company loyalty? Buster lectures me on that once a week. Do you feel loyal to FFC?"

"Haven't thought about it very seriously," Suzy replied with chin in hands. "The way I look at it, a company's just people. Now that you mention it, I hardly know Foley or Feinberg. When I run into Chong, I usually wish I hadn't. As far as my career goes, though, they've provided me with a good environment. I have no complaints."

"You have what it takes, Suzy. Your career would have been just as good with any firm," Clara responded.

This conversation with Clara led Suzy to considerable soul-searching. She doubted if she could accept the kind of guff Clara was taking gracefully. As an officer of the Board of Realtors®, Suzy was becoming friendly with other owners and managers. She began to discern that managerial styles and philosophies are almost as varied as the people who pursue them. Her desire to manage the new branch was now tempered by the thought that there would have to be some in-depth discussion with the bosses before her acceptance.

Meanwhile, Suzy kept her eye on Clara and didn't notice any lessening of the harrassed look or any increase in satisfied purrs. In the end, Clara's career crisis wasn't caused by anything that happened at FFC. It came when she was offered a better job by, of all people, Helga. Helga was running up against all the problems Buster had predicted. She was desperately in need of a manager, so that she could devote her own time to selling. The job offered to Clara promised a higher salary, shorter hours, and more freedom of action. Harry was heard to say that this was equivalent to hitting yourself on the head to take your mind off your aching back. Clara must have had some misgivings about it, too, because she kept deferring the decision.

Clara was still deliberating when another career crisis came to Suzy's attention via an SOS from Eloise.

"I gotta see you right away! It's a matter of life and death!" Eloise shouted into the phone. They arranged to meet for lunch. Eloise's tirade began before Suzy even got inside the door.

"Eight years I've been slaving for that greedy wretch," Eloise screamed, "and he's letting another broker cheat me out of a commission. He won't go to the professional standards committee because the hearings are too time-consuming. Can you believe it?"

"I gather you've had a commission dispute," Suzy said mildly.

"You're damned right I have, and I'm getting about as much support as I get from an old bra."

"So what can you do?" Suzy asked.

"I've done it, baby. He has my letter of resignation on his desk right now. I'm a free woman," Eloise replied with a look of satisfaction.

"Maybe he'll have some second thoughts," Suzy suggested.

"Too late. I wouldn't go back to that wimp if he offered to lick my sidewalk clean. Wish I'd brought you a copy of my letter, Suzy. It was a masterpiece. I worked in every obscenity I know and even invented a few new ones."

"I'll bet. So, now what? Clara'd be thrilled if you'd join us at FFC. We could have fun working together."

"Yes to the fun part, but no to FFC," said Eloise cryptically. "I can't stand big companies. They make me feel like a cheap dress on the marked-down rack."

"You must have something in mind."

"I do. You and me, baby, doing our own thing."

"'You mean start our own company?" Suzy exclaimed. "I should have brought Harry along to tell you about all the pitfalls. Helga's having the same problems. Too much time spent running the show adds up to not enough time for selling."

"I know all that garbage," Eloise replied. "But where is it written that you have to manage a company just because you own it? Managers can be hired."

"Like Helga's trying to hire Clara."

"Exactly. Suzy, haven't you dreamed about working for a broker who's intelligent, interested, and innovative? Well, who's more intelligent and innovative than we are? It's do-it-yourself time. Since you're the superstar, I'll even let you call it Soldsine Realty," said Eloise in her most persuasive tone.

"It's mine, all mine."

"I must say it's got a nice ring to it," Suzy smiled.

Suzy promised to think about it. She drove away feeding on the same dreams she and Marjorie had lovingly nourished when they were planning to open a boutique. By the time she got home, Suzy had pretty well settled on the location and the color scheme, and she was working on the plan for breaking the news to John.

Concurrently, John was working on a plan for breaking some news to Suzy. That his news was important became apparent when he came home with a dozen red roses and invited Suzy out to dinner.

Over the vichyssoise, Suzy said, "I love all this attention for no particular occasion, but I can't help wondering if it's a celebration or a wake."

"I do have something to discuss, and I'm not sure how you'll feel about it," John said, toying with his fork. "I'm not trying to butter you up—or maybe I am."

"Well, if you're planning to run off to Mexico with a hatcheck girl, you can just forget it," Suzy smiled.

"Nothing like that."

"How about just coming out with it before you tear the tablecloth to shreds with that fork," Suzy suggested.

"The company's offered me a district managership, Suzy. It's what I've been gunning for—more responsibility and more pay."

"John that's *terrific!* About time they realized how valuable you are. Why didn't you say so?"

"Because it means we'll be transferred," he blurted.

"Transferred!" Suzy wailed. "You mean leave home—for some godforsaken desert?"

"To Atlanta, Suzy. They don't have deserts in Georgia."

"Swamps, then."

"Look, honey," John said slowly, "I know this is traumatic for you, and probably for the kids, too. I'd hoped for home territory, but you know how big companies operate."

Suzy was speechless. She'd just reached the happy point in her career when clients sought her out and the uncomfortable task of beating the bushes for business was rarely required. Only yesterday, a large retailer had asked her help in relocating 11 transferees.

"We have until June," John went on. "The children can finish the school term before changing. I'll go on ahead to find a new house while you sell the one here. They say the climate's lovely, and we'll make lots of new friends."

"John, are you asking me about this—or telling me?"

"I haven't accepted yet," he replied carefully. "I knew you'd be upset, but I really don't have any choice."

"You damned well do," she exclaimed. "You can just flatly refuse to go."

"And be filed away as a perpetual clerk. That's what happens when you turn down an opportunity like this."

"Well, quit, then, and find another job," Suzy pleaded.

"That'd mean starting all over again on the bottom rung," John explained patiently.

"Isn't that what you're asking me to do?" Suzy cried.

"You can sell houses anywhere, Suzy. Besides, we don't depend on your income for bread and butter."

"But I've worked so hard to get established here," Suzy sniffed, close to tears.

"I knew you'd be upset," John said, patting her hand. "Let's table it for now and sleep on it."

Suzy didn't sleep very well. Never had her house, her job, or her friends seemed so dear. How could one possibly say good-bye to the apple tree that all the kids had climbed? How soon, if ever, in a new city does one find a painless dentist, an honest auto mechanic, or a reliable caterer? Even the thought of leaving mother hurt a little, and the idea of doing without Genevieve was unbearable.

She tossed and turned and argued with herself, rejecting her ingenious schemes for averting the crisis as fast as she thought of them:

SUZY #1: How about if I stay here, and he goes there? We can take turns commuting on weekends. Show business people do it all the time.

SUZY #2: They also get divorced all the time.

SUZY #1: Maybe I should have reminded him that I make more money than he does.

SUZY #2: He knows that. It may be one of the reasons he's gunning for a promotion.

SUZY #1: Maybe I should threaten to quit working, since my contribution's so unimportant.

SUZY #2: Would you like that? I doubt it. You're hooked.

SUZY #1: Maybe he'll change his mind if the kids rise up in rebellion.

SUZY #2: They will, of course, but will you make things easier by encouraging them?

SUZY #1: He's being totally selfish.

SUZY #2: And so are you.

On the following evening, John casually mentioned the proposed move to the children. Mike, who was in the throes of first love, promptly began phoning friends in search of a family who'd board him for 3 years until he finished high school. Erin had a crush on her third grade teacher and burst into inconsolable sobs at the thought that she might never see Mrs. Mullins again. Joey watched the chaos in silence and threw up his supper. Suzy gave up trying to reason with Mike and Erin and settled for mopping up after Joey.

Later, when the kids were bedded down, Suzy said, "John, this decision is just too much. Maybe we should cut the cards to see if we go or stay."

"Oh, that's really terrific," John replied, growing angry. "I've worked my tail off for 15 years to get where I am, and all for this family. So now I'm supposed to cut the cards to see if it should all go down the drain. Apparently, Mike's pimply-faced girlfriend, Erin's teacher, and Suzy's bosses are more important than good old John."

"It isn't the bosses, for heaven's sake, John. Leaving FFC wouldn't bother me a bit. Matter of fact, I was planning to tell you I'm thinking about doing just that."

"To do what?" John asked with very little interest.

"Eloise has resigned from her company, and we had this idea that we might go into business for ourselves."

"Good thing you didn't get past the thinking stage. It wouldn't be a wise move. You and Eloise are terrific saleswomen, but you're not cut out to be administrators."

"Oh, we know that. We plan to be the production line. As a matter of fact," she added with a sudden spurt of inspiration, "we were kind of hoping you might agree to be president of our outfit."

John didn't show a glimmer of interest. In fact, his response was to pick up the Yellow Pages and start jotting down names and numbers of moving companies. Suzy went to bed and fell asleep wondering if she could possibly develop a severe allergy to magnolia blossoms.

On the following day, the whole disastrous situation was reported in detail to Eloise.

"That was a stroke of genius, partner, suggesting that John be president," Eloise bubbled. "I was thinking the same thing. He'd be perfect for the job."

"But he didn't tumble."

"Give it a little time to sink in, hon," Eloise replied. Since when does a super saleswoman assume that *no* means *no?* Didn't happy Hubert teach you about the many faces of *no?*"

"This isn't a sales exercise, damn it," Suzy exclaimed. "John's really hurt, down deep in his male ego—or whatever it is that makes men think women should follow wherever their fearless leaders go. I can't do a selling job on John."

"Course you can't, baby," Eloise said soothingly. "But I can. Put on your hair shirt and your whither-thou-goest mask if you want to, but stall like hell while I get my licks in. I think I'll drop by your house this evening."

Suzy wasn't at all sure that that was a good idea, but Eloise did drop by, armed with a briefcase full of papers.

"John, I may kill you for taking Suzy away," she began. "But before I do that, I need your help. These plans for starting my new company are giving me a monumental headache. How about lending an old friend the benefit of your wisdom?"

"You're really going into this?" he asked incredulously. "Who'll manage it for you? Clara?"

"No, Clara's decided to go back to selling, but she does want to join me. Guess old George'll have to kick the idleness habit and be the boss for a change."

John looked dubious. "Has George ever run an office?"

"George hasn't run anything since his mother sold his electric train set," Eloise replied. "That's why I want your input. This is my estimate for start-up expenses, and this other sheet is a budget for monthly operating costs."

Eloise spread her papers on the coffee table, and John studied them, looking more doubtful all the time.

"This is pretty sketchy, Eloise," he suggested. "No provision for professional services. You'll need a lawyer to draw up incorporation papers. That'll set you back about $1,500. Then you'll need an accountant to set up the books. And you'll have to see an insurance agent."

"Can't stand lawyers and accountants," Eloise cried. "Maybe you could just explain to George what needs to be done. I know this is an imposition, John, but you're so good at this sort of thing."

"Well, let me work on it over the weekend, and I'll see what I can come up with," he agreed.

John worked over the weekend and through the following week. With mounting interest, he withdrew some books on office management and also scrounged some FFC income statements from Clara. He refined and verified his budget figures. Then he drew up a checklist of things to be done and a timetable for doing them. He even drove around to look at potential office locations.

"I've done as much as I can," he said, when Eloise came over for another powwow."

"This is terrific," she replied. "John, I can't tell you how much I appreciate all your effort."

"Well, you may not appreciate the result. It looks too risky, Eloise. Real estate companies go broke at an alarming rate."

"FFC does all right," Suzy said.

"Yes, and that twerp *I* worked for has two Lincoln Continentals, one to use while the other is being serviced," Eloise added.

"Sure, it's possible," John admitted. "But getting started right takes money, and it also takes know-how. The $20,000 you plan to invest wouldn't even get the door open, Eloise. I estimate you should have about $80,000. And you'll need more producers. You and Clara can't carry the overhead alone. As for George managing . . ."

Eloise laughed, "You have a point there, buddy. George would have trouble managing a hopscotch game. Couldn't I raise the money by taking in partners?"

"Yes, that'd probably work," he replied. "This may be a crazy thought, but if Suzy and I, for example, would put up the other $60,000 and take 75 percent of the stock, I'd want to manage the company myself, at least 'till it got on its feet."

"But, John, what about your job? Your promotion?" Suzy exclaimed in disbelief.

"This does solve our dilemma, doesn't it, honey?" he smiled. "We forget about moving, both kiss our jobs good-bye, and start all over on the bottom rung in a whole new venture. What do you think?"

"I think you're a genius," Suzy cried, giving him a hug.

"I'll second the motion," Eloise chimed in gleefully.

"Eloise, could you stand still for our calling it Soldsine Realty?" John asked.

"As someone once said, that has a nice ring to it," she answered.

"You girls'll have to let me be boss, though. If I can't ride herd on your spending habits, we'll be down the tube in no time. We may come a cropper anyhow," John went on.

"We won't—we're born winners," Suzy exulted. "Just don't be upset if we call you Chong by mistake."

Eloise was ecstatic. The children were ecstatic. Clara was ecstatic. Everyone began feverishly working on the plan. Suzy found an office location. Eloise found another. John selected a third. John and Suzy synchronized their watches and resigned their positions simultaneously. Later, they gave a gala emancipation party for a horde of friends. Soldsine Realty, Inc., duly organized, incorporated, registered, insured, and licensed opened its doors for business on a bright, sunny day, just 3 years after Suzy's career had begun.

READER'S QUIZ

This is a guaranteed foolproof quiz. All answers are correct. Give yourself a mark of 100, and brag a lot.

1. Managers of real estate offices can be easily identified by looking for their

    _____ a. cluttered desks.
    _____ b. ink-stained fingers.
    _____ c. frayed cuffs.
    _____ d. gray hairs.
    _____ e. other

2.   Branch managers often complain about the parent company's lack of

_____ a.   communication.
_____ b.   organization.
_____ c.   appreciation.
_____ d.   compensation.
_____ e.   other

3.   I knew it was time to look for another job when

_____ a.   my broker lost his cool.
_____ b.   my broker lost his license.
_____ c.   my desk was moved into the supply room.
_____ d.   the sheriff barred the door.
_____ e.   other

4.   When a career woman's husband is transferred to another city, she can usually

_____ a.   write to NOW.
_____ b.   write to Dear Abby.
_____ c.   write some new resumes.
_____ d.   write him off.
_____ e.   other

5.   The decision to open one's own real estate company is on a par with

_____ a.   a cross-country trip in a 1961 Chevy.
_____ b.   a plunge in the ocean on the first day of spring.
_____ c.   a trek in the jungle, armed with a slingshot.
_____ d.   a decision to spend a week in Las Vegas.
_____ e.   other

14
How Do You Spell "Success"?

Soldsine Realty had truly humble beginnings. John was unconvinced of the importance of walk-in traffic and had selected a second-floor suite with a convenient location, ample parking, and reasonable rent. The building was also decrepit. For the first month the fabulous foursome, as they'd come to call themselves, shared their quarters with assorted carpet layers, carpenters, paper hangers, painters, equipment installers, plumbers, and electricians. Also with an army of fleas, apparently a legacy from an ill-fated pet shop that had once inhabited the first floor.

"No one can say we didn't start from scratch," Eloise said, cheerfully as ever.

Suzy laughed. "May not be an auspicious beginning, but it sure is a noisy one."

"Nothing that can't be remedied," Clara added, vigorously wielding a flyswatter with one hand and a can of insect spray with the other.

With John orchestrating their efforts, all hands pitched in to bring order out of chaos. John had already taken two seminars in office management, but even that couldn't prevent the moments of acute frustration he undoubtedly felt. Nowhere in his studies had they dealt with problems like the water cooler that wouldn't function because of ancient plumbing long since stopped up or rotted away, or a painter who lunches on martinis and develops a whimsical fancy for painting daisies on doors.

Finally, the last worker and the last pile of debris were swept away. The group gazed with pride on their handiwork.

"Gorgeous," Harry proclaimed when he and Frances dropped by. "You've worked a miracle."

"Thanks, but once in a lifetime's enough," Eloise sighed. "My system may never readjust to coffee without sawdust."

"At least we're functional," Suzy said.

"Funky's more like it," Frances giggled. "I adore old buildings. Gosh, the windows even open and shut."

"Yes, and please notice that the plants aren't plastic," John noted.

"What do you think of the location?" Suzy asked anxiously. "I was afraid it might not be quite conspicuous enough."

"Convenient parking beats out a window display by a mile in my book," Harry replied.

Harry was right. In response to announcement ads, a steady stream of friends, fellow brokers, and former clients began dropping in. John hired a receptionist, Junie, who was fresh out of business college and had a talent for keeping phone messages straight and charming the socks off visitors. She had little time for anything else. So, Suzy, Clara, and Eloise took great pleasure in playing tour guide.

John, however, wasn't taking great pleasure in the income statements. Both FFC and Eloise's former employer had wished them luck, but neither had felt charitable about letting any listings go with them. Moreover, the market was in a slump due to a strike at the tractor manufacturing firm, which was the city's major employer. At the end of their first month, no money had come in and no closings were even pending.

"Back to work, ladies," John commanded. "Enough running around for coffee pots and fancy cups. We need some listings."

"But we have to list realistically," Clara said. "Buyers are having a bad case of wait-and-see."

"Does the doctor complain when people are sick?" John asked.

"You have a point there, honey," Suzy smiled.

"Right—and we also need about five more salespeople. Any thoughts on that?"

"Glad you brought that up," Clara added. "We need to grow, I know. But I hope you aren't thinking of grabbing every warm body that comes by."

"I gave up grabbing warm bodies years ago," John laughed. "What I'm getting at is—do we train new people or go after some proven performers?" he asked of the group.

"We could all help train new people," Suzy replied, "but it takes time. A couple of experienced agents wouldn't hurt a bit. Does it violate the code of ethics if we advertise?"

"Hell, no," Eloise snorted. "If it does, Diogenes himself couldn't find an ethical broker. But will that work? I have a feeling an ad would attract a bunch of other brokers' never-satisfieds, and who needs that kind of aggravation?"

"God knows they issue enough licenses—there should be one in every household by now," Clara said. "They might be worth the training hassle if they have promise."

"How can you tell?" Suzy asked.

"Oh, good application forms, interviewing, psychological testing," Clara suggested.

"I have all that," John said. "But I still find myself looking for a common denominator. Take the three of you—different as can be, but the fact remains that you're all good at this job. Why?"

"We all have strong backs, glib tongues, and female hormones. How's that for openers?" Eloise suggested.

"No dice," Suzy interjected. "Harry's an ideal salesman, and he's all male. When he's with a client, he slumps in his chair and chews his pipe. Never says a word. Looks like he's about to fall asleep, but they adore him."

"He's a fantastic listener, and the world needs more of those," Clara agreed.

"That reminds me of training Frances," Suzy smiled. "I thought she'd never learn to tame that runaway mouth."

"So—we look for someone who's either male or female and who can talk a lot or listen a lot—this isn't getting me very far," John complained.

"It's caring that counts," Suzy said thoughtfully. "Caring like crazy for the properties, the people, the work."

"And for the importance of being excellent," Clara added. "Caring with a passion."

"It's like taking on a fireball mistress, my boy," Eloise chimed in. "You have to be more than slightly crazy."

All agreed that Eloise had hit the bull's-eye. The women returned to prospecting, and John sallied forth to look for crazies. Though a sizable number of licensees requested interviews, all proved to be order-takers who were slumping in the falling market and looking for a change of brokers to counteract their lack of selling skills. They were adept at complaining about injustices and finding sources of blame, but they were devoid of passion.

"How goes the new enterprise?" Harry asked Suzy one day when they met for lunch.

"Love our office and our gang, but don't ask me if we've set the market on fire, or I might have to lie a lot," Suzy replied.

"That alone makes you unique among brokers."

"The damned strike really hurts, Harry," she went on. "How are things at FFC?"

"Slumping," Harry replied. "Buster's having another nervous breakdown. Foley's face-lift is sagging. Feinberg still talks in gibberish that only Joel understands."

"And dear Mr. Chong?"

"He's taken to going through our wastebaskets for paper that could be converted to scratch pads."

"Don't tell John about that," Suzy laughed. "It might give him some big ideas."

"Speaking of ideas, FFC's found a dandy way of coping with the recession. They've announced a 'temporary' cut in our commissions."

"A cut?" Suzy exclaimed, increduluous. "Won't that cause a bloody rebellion in the office?"

"It caused me to start thinking about poor old John at the mercy of you three high-powered wenches. In all charity, I just feel that I have to volunteer to help him out. I'm offering my body to Soldsine Realty, Suzy," Harry concluded.

"God, that's marvelous! Body and soul, too? We accept."

"It's a well-known fact that I don't have a soul, but there is one condition."

"Name it, brother. Back-rubs every morning? Irish whiskey in your coffee? Key to the executive john?"

"That too, of course. What I'm getting at, though, is that there's another agent who wants to come along with me. We've developed into quite a team."

"Anyone I know?" Suzy asked.

"Someone you practically gave birth to—gal by the name of Frances."

Suzy let out a joyous whoop. "FFC may start investing in voodoo dolls, but I couldn't be happier if I'd won the sweepstakes. We've all missed you two."

"Then it's a deal?"

"It's a bonanza! John'll be ecstatic."

So John added two more experienced agents to the newly extended family. He also took on three new licensees who offered some signs of incipient insanity. Suzy and Clara assisted in implementing a training program. The listing inventory grew, and Soldsine "sold" signs began sprouting like toadstools after a heavy rain.

The tractor strike continued. With fixed overhead and more people producing business, though, the company forged past its break-even point and into black ink 2 months ahead of John's projection. John himself accounted for the sale of a large warehouse. They began looking into the establishment of a profit-sharing trust. Suzy and John were working themselves to a frazzle and enjoying every minute of it.

"Can't you guys talk about anything but real estate?" Mike complained one night at dinner.

"Was it more exciting when I talked about earth compounders?" John asked mildly.

"Or when I babbled about how much whiter the sheets got when I hung them outside to dry?" Suzy added.

"I wanna talk about my teacher," Erin commanded.

"What about your teacher?" they asked.

"She stinks. I wish we'd moved to Atlanta. I wish they'd held me back so I could still have Mrs. Mullins."

Suzy'd counted it a blessing when Erin got over starting every sentence with "Mrs. Mullins says . . . ." Suzy reassured her, "You'll get used to Miss Sparks."

"The kids have a point," John told Suzy later. "We're so wrapped up in the business that we never get away from it."

"Having a time management problem, darling?" Suzy asked innocently.

"Ouch. Apparently I am. The kids seem to feel neglected, and so does my bowling ball."

They joined a bowling league, took the kids on a weekend camping trip, and gave a series of small dinner parties. In a temporary frenzy of parental guilt, John and Joey became Indian Guides and Suzy agreed to direct the fourth grade play. Suzy also accepted the chairmanship of the local United Fund drive. They restored some balance to their lives, but their hearts were still in the company.

Finally, the strike was settled, and the market picked up. The meteoric rise of Soldsine Realty was the talk of the town. All of the regulars were having a great year, and two of the novices were producing consistently. The third had, at John's subtle suggestion, joined a competitor. More licensees were clamoring to join, and the original space was bursting at the seams. A second clerk joined Junie, and John began looking for a location for their first branch. He prevailed upon Clara to have another go at branch management.

"Well, it's time to talk about a first anniversary celebration," John announced one day at a sales meeting. "The traditional awards banquet."

"That's a great tradition for breaking," Harry said slowly. "Especially the monkey suits. How about a clambake on the beach?"

"Why not make the plaques out of pizza dough?" Eloise added. "That way, they're good for something."

"I hate awards, period," Frances offered. "Makes one or two people feel wonderful, and the rest feel like second-class citizens. Suzy's won enough awards. Let's concentrate on booby prizes."

"Maybe we're too small a group to make it meaningful," Clara suggested. "Let's skip the prizes and just go out on the town for a first-class steak."

Suzy and John decided to have the party in their home, and they gave prizes to everyone. Also plaques made out of pizza dough. The attire was informal, and no one was allowed to make a speech. A new tradition was born, and judging from the fun they all had, it was bound to flourish.

That isn't to say that John's tuxedo was allowed to gather moths. The whole staff dressed up in their best glad rags to attend the annual banquet of the state Association of Realtors®. There was the usual well-attended open bar, followed by mediocre food and innocuous speeches. The highlight of the evening was the announcement of the "Realtor of the Year." The presenter tantalized them with a 10-minute speech full of carefully screened hints.

"Our 'Realtor of the Year' is, as always, a person who represents the highest ethical standards of our profession," he began.

"That's debatable," Harry whispered.

"And one who's given unstintingly of time and talent to the association and to the community." The room was beginning to buzz.

"Probably the retiring president, as usual," Suzy thought.

"I'm happy to say that this year's winner represents our new and growing youthful segment," the presenter went on.

"That lets Foley out," Frances giggled.

"And also represents the fair sex."

This was greeted by a gasp of surprise and a hasty replacing of bets. By the time the punch line was reached, everyone in the room except Suzy Soldsine had rightly put down money on *Suzy Soldsine*. She was flabbergasted. She didn't even remember to slip on her shoes and walked to the podium in stocking feet. Accepting an enormous bouquet of roses, blinking at flashbulbs, and gulping for air, she said:

"This is unreal!"

"Is that the sum total of your acceptance speech?" the presenter teased.

"Are you kidding? I accept—and thank you, thank you, thank you. Wish I could think of all the people I'm especially grateful to, but right now I can't even remember my own name. I should share this, though, with one Realtor who's believed in me and straightened out my messes. Also cleaned the gumdrops off my typewriter and fathered my children. After all, I'm only half of the Soldsine team."

Much later, the Soldsine group gathered for hamburgers and coffee at Dino's.

"We're so proud of you, Suzy," Frances cried. "You've done it all, achieved every goal we can aspire to. You're Mrs. Success. Now just figure out how to bottle the formula so we can all have a dose."

"You've defined it yourself," Clara said. "Success is establishing goals and reaching them. Then setting new goals."

"Lots of people have goals, but very few have the capacity for going after them with the single-minded drive of a good bird dog after a fat pheasant," Harry suggested.

"Here we go again—back to defining what makes a superstar," exclaimed John. He was beaming with pride, and Suzy was quietly crying into her dill pickle.

"You're all so good to me, but I'm not really all that special," she sniffed. "I've had a lot of lucky breaks."

"Luck, schmuck," Eloise cried. "You're terrific, Suzy, and I demand the credit for having brought you into this crazy business. Someday I plan to write a book about your career."

"Do you really write books?" Frances asked.

"I have, and I will again when I find the time," Eloise replied.

"That's it," John said suddenly.

"That's what?" they all asked.

"The margin of difference that makes a person a superstar. Eloise said it—the word *someday.*"

"Some people have all the luck."

"If you can boil the formula for success down into a single word, I'll have it tattooed on my fanny," Eloise remarked. "But I don't get the connection between *success* and *someday*."

"The point is," John explained, "Suzy doesn't know that word exists. She doesn't have any *someday* goals. If the goal's not worth the effort, she puts it clean out of her mind. If it is, she goes after it *now*."

"The *someday* people are dreamers," Harry agreed. "The *now* people are winners. *Now* should fit nicely on one cheek, Eloise."

"Hey, gang, remember Murphy's Law?" Frances asked excitedly.

"If anything can possibly go wrong, it will," Clara dutifully recited.

"Right. Well, now let's proclaim Suzy's Law."

"Which is . . . ?" they all chorused.

"That Murphy's full of beans!"

On the following day, Soldsine Realty returned to normal, which is to say an average degree of chaos. John wrestled with quarterly income tax returns, while Suzy called on a developer to try and list a condominium project. Clara sketched floor plans for her new office, and Frances went out to ring doorbells. Harry quit smoking and became extremely touchy. Eloise placed a ream of white paper beside her typewriter and rolled a sheet into place. Smiling, she typed "The Saga of Suzy Soldsine, page 1."

READER'S QUIZ

This is a guaranteed foolproof quiz. All answers are correct. Give yourself a mark of 100, and brag a lot.

1.   The hardest step in opening my new office was

_____ a.   finding a location with enough electrical outlets.
_____ b.   getting permission to reserve the elevator for my moving men.
_____ c.   convincing my landlord that my computer terminal wouldn't leak radiation.
_____ d.   paying the bills.
_____ e.   other

2.   When recruiting a new sales staff, good prospects are likely to be found in

_____ a.   other brokers' offices.
_____ b.   a vacuum cleaner company.
_____ c.   the unemployment office.
_____ d.   the divorce court.
_____ e.   other

3. I'll never aspire to win

   _____ a.   a Nobel Prize.
   _____ b.   an Academy Award.
   _____ c.   the presidency of General Motors.
   _____ d.   a battle with a utility company.
   _____ e.   other

4. I knew I was successful when

   _____ a.   my exhusband stopped paying alimony.
   _____ b.   my banker invited me to lunch.
   _____ c.   my bookie let me run a tab.
   _____ d.   my mother-in-law remembered my birthday.
   _____ e.   other

5. Success is

   _____ a.   fame and fortune.
   _____ b.   fiction.
   _____ c.   fantasy.
   _____ d.   fattening.
   _____ e.   other